❧ THE SERMONS OF THE CURÉ OF ARS

"Some people are so profoundly ignorant that they do not recognize a quarter of their ordinary sins."

—The Curé of Ars
Page 35

St. John-Baptiste-Marie Vianney (1786-1859), popularly known as the Curé of Ars. He was pastor (curé) at Ars, a small farmer's village about 20 miles north of Lyons, France from 1818 till his death in 1859. His incorrupt body reposes over one of the altars in the Basilica at Ars.

THE SERMONS
OF THE
CURÉ OF ARS

Translated by
UNA MORRISSY
*with a special Foreword to
the English translation by*
LANCELOT SHEPPARD

*"Alas, poor religion, how little is known of
you."*

—The Curé of Ars
Page 67

TAN BOOKS AND PUBLISHERS, INC.
Rockford, Illinois 61105

Nihil Obstat: Jacobus Canonicus Bastible
                Censor Deputatus

Imprimatur: ✠ Corelius
                Episcopus Corcagiensis et Rossensis
                Corcagiensis
                die 10 Augustii, 1959

Type reproduced by arrangement with Henry Regnery Company, a subsidiary of Eagle Publishing, Washington, D.C.

Previously published as *Sermons de Jean-Baptiste-Marie Vianney, pauvre curé d'Ars* by Le Club du Livre Chrétien, Paris.

Library of Congress Catalog Card No.: 95-60486

ISBN: 0-89555-524-7

Printed and bound in the United States of America.

TAN BOOKS AND PUBLISHERS, INC.
P.O. Box 424
Rockford, Illinois 61105
1995

"When all is said and done, there is not a single person who could say that he is ready to appear before Jesus Christ. Yet in spite of the fact that we are quite aware of this, there is still not one among us who will take a single step nearer to God. Dear Lord, how blind the sinner is! How pitiable is his lot! My dear children, let us not live like fools any longer, for at the moment when we least expect it, Jesus Christ will knock at our door. How happy then will be the person who has not been waiting until that very moment to prepare himself for Him."

—The Curé of Ars

Page 25

"*Generally speaking, one dies as one has lived. That is one of the great truths which Holy Scripture and the Fathers repeat in many different places. If you live as good Christians, you will be sure to die as good Christians, but if you live badly, you will be sure to die a bad death . . . It is true, however, that sometimes, by a kind of miracle, one may begin badly and finish well, but that happens so rarely that, as St. Jerome puts it, death is generally the echo of life. You think that you will return then to God? No, you will perish in sin. . .*"

—The Curé of Ars
Page 139

PUBLISHER'S PREFACE

The Sermons of the Curé of Ars constitutes one of the most insightful, penetrating and moving Saints' writings possessed by the Church. Yet St. John-Baptiste-Marie Vianney (1786-1859—known popularly as "The Curé of Ars") has an undeserved reputation among some people for having been unintelligent and unlearned. Moreover, in reading the original Foreword, Introduction and Afterword of this book—which have been retained in this edition because they are so instructive—one could possibly gain the mistaken notion that the holy Curé's sermons are mostly copied from others more learned than himself and more competent to write. Further, the reader could gain another mistaken notion from these prefatory and following commentaries that the Curé of Ars was too severe (as when he railed against dancing), even to the point of being Jansenistic. The purpose of this brief Preface is to refute these four errors, as well as to attempt to apprise the reader in advance as to the nature and value of the *Sermons of the Curé of Ars.*

St. John Vianney grew up as a farm worker and by the age of 19 had had only some two years of formal education. He had been conscripted into the Napoleonic army and was marching off to fight in Spain when he had to fall out, due to illness, and take succor and healing in a nearby town. As a result, he never saw military service, whereas he might well have been killed during Napoleon's disastrous Spanish campaign, as were so many thousands of Frenchmen. When he attempted seminary after the wars, therefore, he was ill-equipped to handle the studies, which in those days were entirely in Latin. Latin is a particularly difficult language, which many a good soul has struggled to master without success. King Philip II of Spain (1527-1598) tried unsuccessfully for competence in it in order to be able the better to read diplomatic correspondence. And no one has ever criticized Philip II for being stupid.

That a person with just two years of formal education before his priestly training would be unlearned in school subjects only stands to reason, but St. John Vianney was definitely NOT unlearned in the Faith. One need only go to Ars to see his library, which constitutes two large bookcases. He continually applied himself to the study of our holy religion, especially in theology, that he might be completely accurate in his sermons. And, one need only read these present sermons to verify this point. They demonstrate a total familiarity with the Faith and a great degree of learning therein—even though composed by a young priest in his early thirties.

Abbé Francis Trochu, a great, great authority on the Curé of Ars and author of the definitive biography, *The Curé D'Ars,* tends to indicate in his Afterword to the present volume that many of these sermons—or at least large parts of them—were copied from those of others. Not trying to gainsay the learned Abbé Trochu, still I feel it must be said that these sermons are *entirely* the sermons of the Curé of Ars. For they all bear the same identical mark or quality of his unique insight and character. They are, that is, the predigested thought and understanding of one great, single-minded, holy intellect in his attempt to instruct his subjects in the Faith. The palpable impress of the Curé's mind stamps every word of them—the interior evidence of this fact from the sermons themselves is unmistakable. And thus, though it is instructive to know where he obtained his sermon matter, the reason these sermons are pure gold is the fact they have been refined in a great Saint's heart. What in part might have begun as another's ideas have been converted into the ideas of but one man. Therefore, these ARE, truly, the sermons of the Curé of Ars.

A case could be made, I believe, that in every epoch of the Church there exists a popular, common cast of thought vis-à-vis interpreting the Faith for the common people. To the extent that this is so, it might be said that the era immediately preceding the Curé of Ars hinted of severity, that being the time of the Jansenist heresy—a heresy basically of severity. St. John Vianney is sometimes accused of severity—even to the point of being Jansenistic—especially, for example, as regards dancing, which, in its legitimate forms, the Church has never condemned, but allows.

On this point, one must realize that the insights of a great Saint are born out of a constant, holy, prayerful and (in St. John Vianney's case) priestly study of "the faith of God." (*Rom.* 3:3). Such a man becomes a "prophet" in the truest sense—that of one who knows the truth and exposes it for others to understand. Such a man can appear severe because he *knows*—and others do not—the truth regarding the all-importance of salvation ("For what doth it profit a man if he gain the whole world and suffer the loss of his own soul?"—*Matt.* 16:26) and the difficulty of attaining it ("If thy right hand scandalize thee, cut it off, and cast it from thee: for it is expedient for thee that one of thy members should perish, rather than that thy whole body go into hell."—*Matt.* 5:30). Has anyone ever accused our dear and gentle Saviour of being severe when He spoke these and other comparable strong words? Of course not.

Further, what shall we think of the Old Testament when

it says, "It is better to die without children, than to have ungodly children." (*Ecclus.* 16:4)? Is this not a most dire warning to parents of their tremendous duties toward their children? Or what of the New Testament when it says, "It is better to marry than to be burnt." (*1 Cor.* 7:9)? Can we accuse Sacred Scripture of severity, of Jansenism? Ridiculous! The facts are these: Salvation is *all-important,* and the way thereto a big, difficult job, a lifetime job, one fraught with many and various pitfalls. "And if the just man shall scarcely be saved, where shall the ungodly and the sinner appear?" (*1 Peter* 4:18). St. John Vianney could rejoinder such criticisms of severity with the words of the Apostle, "Am I then become your enemy because I tell you the truth?" (*Gal.* 4:16). The Curé of Ars is merely telling us the truth. And the truth is tough—yes, even a bit severe! But does this mean that dancing is in fact wrong, that the Church is wrong in allowing it? Or that St. John Vianney is wrong in condemning it? No, in both cases. It only means that, in the case of the Curé of Ars' condemnation of dancing, for his people the practice was luring souls away from God, and thus he was right to excoriate it. Among the many, many prophecies about the Great Catholic Monarch, incidentally, is one that says he will eliminate dancing. Why? The answer is easy. Just consider what passes today for dancing. Some of it is pure lasciviousness. To today's depraved neo-pagans, could a lawgiver say that *this* type of dancing is all right, but *that* is not? Would not wisdom, rather, dictate eliminating the practice of dancing altogether, so that the flame of passion already fired within the breasts of so many of the world's population might be allowed—from the provocation of dancing at least—to cool and die down? Dancing, the Curé perceived, was leading his people to Hell by diverting them from their religion and leading them into mortal sin. The practice of dancing *per se* is not bad, but in that historical context it apparently needed to be condemned. And he condemned it.

What exactly are *The Sermons of the Curé of Ars* as presented in this edition? They are a number of things: First of all, they are only *excerpts* from the some eighty-five extant sermons of the Saint. The complete sermons are quite a bit longer and constitute a considerably larger book than the present one. Probably this edition should have been called *The Best of the Sermons of the Curé of Ars,* because, for popular reading, these selections are more easily digested and page for page more provocative and more moving, since they distill much of the essence of the complete sermons.

They constitute, moreover, as Abbé Trochu points out, only the early sermons of the man of God, those he wrote out at the beginning of his priestly career at Ars, when, being unsure of himself as a preacher, he had to provide himself the prop of a prepared, written text. But for this, they are all the more remarkable because they were written when he was a relatively young man, which tells us something profound about the level of his sanctity. Judging from these sermons, he was already a Saint as a young priest!

These sermons, moreover, were written for a lax parish, one that had been without a priest for some time. They are phrased to jar a spiritually complacent people from their lethargy—to blast them into consciousness about the reality of their situation. Therefore, they are strong— strongly worded, penetratingly pointed at man's own spiritual self-deception. They expose the myriad ways we hide our sinful habits from our own attention. They are construed to crack away the crust we build up around our voluptuous self-comfort. They are at times not very pleasant to read because they shine the light of truth into the hidden recesses of our spiritual self-satisfaction, showing us where we are wrong. Facing the truth about ourselves is never really pleasant, especially where we do not want to admit it.

In respect to their subtlety and spiritual sophistication, these sermons will come as quite a surprise to most readers. And one will not conclude a reading of this book without the realization he has come into contact with a profound, a holy, a great and powerful mind, one imbued totally with the love of God, the knowledge of the Faith and the welfare of souls. These writings, though in some slight respect dated and provincial, bear overall the timeless and classic imprint of the essence of Catholicism. Thus, they are timely for today and for all times. Perhaps they are especially suited to our own era, when so much of our Catholic tradition has been jettisoned and is eschewed—even by some of the Catholic clergy—and many of the sheep of Christ as a result have gone to graze in secular and even heretical pastures. That Catholics of our time have lost the dual perception of the importance of salvation and the demands of the task is understandable. Few sermons ever speak of it. But the Curé of Ars does.

From the little French country village to which he was seemingly consigned to an unknown oblivion, the words of a prophet of God emerge from a few score of his early sermons—which yet could have a greater total impact on the world than his incredible pastoral ministry, for which he has become so duly famous and which has won him the Church's accolade, "Patron Saint of Parish Priests." For out of these sermons pulses the heart of the Saint, instructing, converting, speaking . . . with an immediacy, an intimacy and an urgency that, in my opinion, no other Saint in history has equalled. When one reads his spiritual thoughts, culled from his writings and sayings, one soon realizes he has encountered a simplicity and a power in religious expression that are exceeded only by the Bible.

Ars is located some twenty miles or so north of Lyons, which is a major city situated in the center of France. Ars lies eight or ten miles east of the main road from Lyons to Paris. As in St. John Vianney's time, so today, to get to Ars, one has to *want* to go there. Yet, in his own lifetime, some 300 people a day came to Ars—over 100,000 a year! A special coach service from Lyons had to be established to accommodate all the pilgrims. Why? To provide the world access to a man of God, to a man who had been unable to manage regular seminary training, to a man seemingly given the humblest of all the humble parishes of the world, to a man who one would have thought would now be long forgotten by all. People came *then* by the thousands to see a man who had said to the little boy who pointed out for him the way to Ars when he first approached it to take up his role as pastor: "You have shown me the way to Ars; I will show you the way to Heaven."

Today the pilgrims come by the tens of thousands to this remote village—over half a million people a year, including even the present Pope, to make the pilgrimage to a place where a poor, emaciated man made holy history and from which he still teaches—now the world—in the form of his sermons and holy sayings.* Most of us will never have the chance to go to Ars, but every one of us can open himself to receive the holy wisdom of St. John Vianney contained in this book of his sermons and let the saintly Curé of Ars now show *us* the way to Heaven.

Thomas A. Nelson, Publisher
August 5, 1995
Feast of Our Lady of the Snows

———

* See the booklet *Thoughts of the Curé D'Ars* (TAN, 1984).

"Let us try hard, my dear brethren, to destroy all that could be in the smallest way displeasing to Jesus Christ, and we shall see how our Communions will help us to make great strides towards Heaven. And the more we do this, the more we shall feel ourselves becoming detached from sin and inclining towards God."

—The Curé of Ars
Page 138

FOREWORD

Of all the sermons that are preached in the Church throughout the world how few are published. Priests labor to instruct and inspire their flocks to a better life; they preach Sunday after Sunday—many priests more than once on a Sunday—and most of these efforts go unrecorded, for the sermon is an ephemeral and short-lived composition; even more than a newspaper story, it is dead immediately it has been preached. And the sermon needs to be fitted to its audience, it must be in terms that are understood, it must be of its own times, and in an idiom suited to those it is intended to influence. Consequently, the few sermons that are published, usually those by famous preachers, speak to people of the present; the voices of dead preachers rarely come to us by the printed word, or if they do how seldom do they move us. And if this is true of men of one's own country and language, how much more true it is of those not only from a past century but from another country, who spoke another language, who preached under conditions and within a context that never could have been ours.

Yet in this book we have a selection of sermons from the pen of a man who died just a century ago, a parish priest in a small agricultural village just north of Lyons in France, to which he was appointed in 1818, three years after Napoleon's downfall. They are the sermons he preached to his little flock endeavoring to make them better Christians, before the time came when he could speak of his parish as completely converted.

To appreciate these sermons, therefore, our first task is to put them back into their context—the context of the life of the man who preached them and of those whom he addressed. Most readers are probably acquainted with the main facts of the life of the preacher, St. John Vianney, the Curé d'Ars, and know that when he was appointed to Ars he came to a parish that, owing to the French Revolution and the shortage of priests, had been neglected for many years, a place where very few of the people went to Mass on Sundays or made their Easter duties. We have to remember also that the Curé d'Ars was not a learned man and that he had been sent away from the seminary because he knew so little Latin that he could not follow the course of lectures. He was obliged to study his theology from a book (the *Rituel de Toulon*) that in reality was not a theological treatise at all; it was a handy "Inquire Within upon Everything" for the busy parish priest which told him the minimum that he had to know to run his parish, what his duties were, what his rights, and gave a summary of the dogmatic and moral theology that would be all that he might be expected to need.

We also know how by dint not of his persuasive speech but by the mute eloquence of his holy life he converted his parish and indeed attracted to it thousands from all over the world so that in the last year of his life (1858-9) something like a hundred thousand persons made the journey to Ars. But they did not come for his preaching but to consult him in the confessional and to lay their troubles at his feet, perhaps even to ask for a miracle (and there were miracles at Ars). Yet they would have heard him preach, quite informally at the morning instruction that he gave every day or, at greater length, on Sundays.

These were not the sermons that we can now read. Then he had not time to prepare and write them down besieged as he was by day and by night, at the mercy of the countless pilgrims. It was in his early days as a priest at Ars that he prepared his sermons, writing them all down beforehand and learning them by heart. These in the main are the sermons of his that we have; what few morsels of his later pulpit utterances have come down to us have done so from the pens of others who put down what they remembered and unconsciously perhaps polished what they reported.

In those early days at Ars its young parish priest had to bring his people back to the practice of their religion. And there is the first difference between those days and our own, for his problems are not exactly the problems of the priest today. Nowadays the great obstacle is not so much morality as faith; priests have to preach the faith, to kindle the spark that through grace will cause men to believe in God and the teaching of the Church. In Ars at the beginning of the nineteenth century St. John Vianney was confronted with a flock that possessed the faith but were exceedingly lax in its practice; it had grown dim no doubt but it was there and for that reason his task was easier for morality in general is a consequence of belief. He preached therefore principally on morality, the sinfulness of dancing and drinking (the besetting sins of the people of Ars), the need to reform, the terrors of hell, the joys of heaven. Reading these efforts nowadays we are at once struck by their severity, their seeming lack of compassion and indeed what we are tempted to call their Jansenistic approach. We know that St. John Vianney was a saint and therefore *ex hypothesi* no Jansenist. He certainly did not preach heresy nor condone it, but he followed scrupulously the practice of his times and in taking his teaching from the approved sources of those days inevitably presented it in a form that was colored by a contemporary approach and preoccupations. It will help us to realize this more clearly if we examine the method of composition that he used and the sources from which he took his sermons.

How did he prepare for what was a considerable ordeal for him on those Sunday mornings? We know that his sermons cost him an enormous effort and that he prepared them with immense care. With the aid of certain works of reference he wrote out his sermons at length. He had never been much good at his books and the effort at actual composition, for he wrote out every word, took him some time. Occasionally he would leave the sacristy, where he wrote on the vestment press, and go to kneel before the altar. Hours were spent in this way in the preparation of a sermon and once it was all down on paper he set about learning it by heart, thirty or forty pages of it covered with his spidery, unformed handwriting, with never a paragraph and hardly a margin. His memory had always been poor. When he thought that he had mastered his sermon he would try it over in the churchyard out aloud late on Saturday night and more than once, to his embarrassment, passers-by caught him in the act.

The congregation that at the beginning of his pastorate at Ars came to hear these sermons was scanty enough—a few old peasant women, the lady of the manor, perhaps a couple of men and some of the children. And the new parish priest made so much noise that they could not go to sleep while he preached. He shouted and declaimed. After the Gospel at the sung Mass on Sunday mornings, when he put off his chasuble and went up the rickety wooden steps to the pulpit, they knew that he would be there for a good hour, that they would be forced to listen and that they would hear nothing for their comfort.

Examples of these sermons of his early days at Ars are still extant. In later years, when he ceased to write them down beforehand and preached, not without preparation—his entire life was that—but without the set form that he at first adopted, the whole style was changed. In those first months as a parish priest he preached to his flock about the proper way to behave in church, about keeping Sunday holy and the purpose of his work in Ars as their priest which was, he told them, to lead them all to heaven. His instructions were moral rather than dogmatic; dancing, the frequentation of taverns, Sunday work, earned his severest reproofs.

There were occasions when he lost the thread of his sermons, stumbled over a phrase and, remembering no more, was obliged to leave the pulpit. After a short night, worn out with his efforts to learn it all by heart, chronically undernourished and still fasting at perhaps nearly eleven of a Sunday morning, he could hardly have expected it otherwise. There came a time when, caught in the pulpit and remembering nothing of his carefully prepared discourse, he began to improvise and in doing so found himself as a preacher.

The complete written sermons of the Curé d'Ars number eighty-five; taken as a whole they are extremely revealing on the subject of the preacher. This point can hardly be explored here for a whole biography would be needed for the purpose. What is more to the point in our present context is to examine the sources laid under contribution by the Curé d'Ars and the extent of his indebtedness to them.

A careful textual examination of the Curé's sermons reveals the use that he made of other sources. He had a few sermon manuals, nearly all of which he acquired before 1830. Some few sermons are copied out almost verbatim from Bonnardel's "familiar instructions," others come from Msgr. Joly's "Prones," but here the Curé was more discriminating. He was prepared to follow his author into the high-flown oratory (that, one may imagine, came strangely from the lips of this simple country parish priest), but when Msgr. Joly became involved in learned and intricate theological discussion there his follower abandoned him not, as a rule, to write something of his own but to seek in another, more homely source (possibly the missionary sermons of Lajeune or Cochin's book) the application and explanation of the point that he was trying to make.

Rodriguez' book figures among those at Ars but it does not seem to have been used as a source save for anecdotes (those who are familiar with this classic on Christian perfection will remember that it is crammed with them, and they read strangely to modern ears). It has been said that the sermon on humility came from the Curé's mastery of Rodriguez' treatment of that subject, but we now know that this sermon came from another source.

It is interesting to notice that if the Curé d'Ars was indebted to Bonnardel the good canon himself was not above doing a little copying: he took the Sunday sermons of one Reguis (the book figures in the library at Ars) of something like half a century earlier and endowing them with a trifle more concision and a more polished literary style gave them to the public. Bonnardel was humble enough to say whence his material came. Most of the Curé's sermons owe something to Bonnardel and several are an anthology of passages taken from this book but from different sermons. One of the Curé's characteristic sermons on "the sanctification of the Christian," considered for long as one of his most personal efforts, comes almost entirely from Bonnardel's "How to behave throughout the year."

The Curé's other favorite source was the (anonymous) *Catechiste des Peuples.* Here he found the matter of something like twenty sermons and, unlike Bonnardel's book, plenty of anecdotes to drive home the points. If some of the sermons reveal that, apart from a few reflections, whole long passages were copied, others, it must be acknowledged, show that several sources were laid under contribution, that points were arranged differently from the treatment in the original and that in some cases the preacher's own contribution was somewhat more extensive than in other instances, though it was never very great.

What are we to make of all this? The published sermons of the Curé's are priceless evidence of what he thought appropriate for the people of his parish in the early years of the nineteenth century. If they show us nothing else they are, we can be certain, the *choice* that he made, and even this small indication reveals to us something of the man. Then, too, they are evidence of his humility. He was neither learned nor eloquent and indeed, save in the technical sense, he was hardly literate (examination of his manuscripts and letters shows this clearly) but he knew what he was about and by his life and preaching successfully inculcated the "one thing necessary" and changed the whole face of his village so that what had been almost the worst and the least regarded parish in the diocese, became the model for the whole country and drew to it thousands upon thousands of pilgrims from all over the world.

So these sermons, put together with such labor have something to tell us, even if it is not what we expect. We can still read what the Curé *said* on those Sunday mornings that proved so hard an ordeal for him and if we find in many of his utterances "naught for our comfort" we can still obtain some reassurance from the fact that it was the Curé's purpose to jolt his people out of their laxity—perhaps he will do the same for us.

There remains then the question of the Curé's alleged rigorism which has been dubbed Jansenistic. This can be disposed of quite shortly. There is no doubt that in certain matters (deferment of absolution, postponement of first communions, his extreme abhorrence of dancing, his diatribes against taverns, for example) he appears to qualify for such an epithet. But before we go so far there are certain points to be borne in mind. Take first the usual practice prevailing at that time in the diocese where he worked. A catechism in circulation in 1818 puts the age for first communion at between eleven and thirteen years of age, especially in boarding schools; it appears clearly enough from the context that children in the countryside might have to wait until even later when they were properly instructed and had "given proof of their perseverance in virtue." Read the moral theology treatise in use in the seminary at Lyons at the beginning of the nineteenth century—it was not used by St. John Vianney because it was in Latin and he could not follow the classes in that language. This book, by Bailly, displays a rigorism that seems to us nowadays to be quite impossible. (It is interesting that the book was later condemned, but it was nevertheless a mirror of the practice current at that time.) The *Rituel de Toulon* (the Curé's makeshift theology course) was of a similar nature. The trend of the times was towards severity (compare the fasting rules in France or even in the U.S.A. then and now) and an arid legalism that strikes us at the present time as devoid of encouragement for men on their road to heaven.

Doctrinally Jansenism was dead—in *practice* some of its effects lived on. But it is too easy to term Jansenistic all that strikes us nowadays as too hard for man to bear. We have only to read the lives of the saints of those days or indeed of the last three hundred years to see that while moral principles remain constant their application in a given situation undergoes variations of emphasis. Read St. Francis de Sales on dancing, study a little of St. Benedict Joseph Labre's attitude to everything (in his view) concerning chastity, consider what some doctors of the Church have said about the theatre and then reflect on our times, not on their specifically evil manifestations but on those things that we take for granted—parish dances, card parties, theatrical entertainments and the like. We have our difficulties and grievous temptations but it is probable, I think, that if another saint like the Curé d'Ars arose in our midst the things that he would castigate might well lie elsewhere, things, possibly, that have not occurred to us.

That the Curé d'Ars may have used a severity in dealing with his flock that now appears foreign to our present habits is really unimportant; he was of his times, he spoke to them in their own idiom, but we should not forget that as years went on his severity diminished and, though dancing remained his especial aversion, he did not defer absolution as he had previously done, and the burden of his sermons—copied from no one: he had not the time—welled up from a heart overflowing with love of God. That is just another way of saying that as a young priest his steps were firmly set on the path to heaven but he had not come to the heights of holiness; when as an old man he stood in his pulpit, toothless and mumbling so that few could hear him, the burden of his message was the love of God and the very sight of him standing there moved many to tears and contrition. His sermon was his life. But he had reached the goal of sanctity principally through his devotion to duty as a parish priest, and that duty had included preparing sermons as *best he could* for his erring parishioners in those far-off days; for he realized well his limitations. And that is only one of the lessons of that incredible life of his: devotion to duty that led him to heaven and, we may be sure, many of his flock with him.

Lancelot C. Sheppard

INTRODUCTION

THE Curé of Ars knew no vanity whatsoever, not even the vanity of authorship. All he had printed during his lifetime were "four or five prayers dictated to Mlle. Lassagne, the directress of *La Providence*,"[1] and even these appeared under the veil of anonymity in the *Guide for Pious Souls*, a work which was sometimes attributed to him, but which was really that of a priest from Lyons, M. l'Abbé Peyronnet, chaplain at Fourvière.[2]

If Jean-Baptiste-Marie Vianney had wished to give something to the public, undoubtedly he would have chosen to publish his sermons, of which he had completed easily six volumes. The thought never even occurred to him. He kept his manuscripts for a certain number of years, perhaps as long as he hoped that he would be able to use them again. But the time came—around 1832 or so—when, overwhelmed by the work of the confessional, he no longer had even the leisure to reread his manuscripts, and he did not give any further thought to them.

He had a good hundred sermons. He had put them away on a shelf in his bookcase when, towards 1845, Canon Perrodin, the Superior of the seminary at Brou, in the diocese of Belley, who was preparing a spiritual book, borrowed the Curé's instructions which had dealt either with the life of our Lord or with the Blessed Sacrament.[3] Most unfortunately, irreparable damage was done, for this series of sermons was lost in the following way:

When Canon Perrodin wanted to return to M. Vianney the twenty copies of sermons which he had taken he could not at once meet with him, for the Curé was in the confessional and would be there for many hours to come. He entrusted them to M. Raymond, who was the assistant to the Curé of Ars between 1845 and 1853.

The Abbé Raymond kept them. Though he was perfectly convinced of the exalted virtue of M. Vianney he privately considered him gifted with only a modest eloquence. He had not, therefore, any idea of making use of someone else's sermons. Nor had his pastor any need for his old manuscripts: having no time to prepare anything, the holy man was at present delivering his sermons and catechisms *ex tempore*. M. Raymond shoved the scripts away in a drawer. When in 1853 he was appointed pastor at Jayat, he threw them in among a pile of papers that were of no importance. As a witness at the Beatification Process on February 24, 1863, he admitted to this: "I had twenty sermons of the Servant of God, but I lost them."

With regard to the manuscript sermons of M. Vianney which escaped destruction—about eighty-five in number—they are no longer in Ars.

No doubt because they had begged him for them, he had given a certain number of them to the Brothers of the Holy Family at Belley, founders of the school, or workers at the church in Ars; others he had *sold* to Mlle. Marie Ricotier. This lady, born in Gleize (Rhône), retired in 1832 to the village of Ars, where she lived on a small private income. M. Vianney was often short of money and Mlle. Ricotier, to come to his help in his charitable works and also—as she admitted—to procure very surreptitiously for herself, during the very lifetime of the saint, some honored relics, bought from him all the souvenirs possible: furniture, worn out vestments, and so on. It is very possible that Mlle. Ricotier suggested to the Abbé Vianney that he had in his room some manuscripts which were of no value and that she quite willingly gave him hard cash in exchange for them. The holy man never had enough of it for the poor. Whatever the explanation, a large number of the sermons disappeared that way—as relics—into the hands of this very far-seeing parishioner.[5]

The Abbé Claude Rougemont, missionary of the diocese of Belley, who was appointed pastor of Ars in 1871, declared at the *Process* (Session of March 5, 1886): "according to Catherine Lassagne and Brother Athanasius, director of the school, when he was sending his sermons to M. Colomb, the Servant of God had forbidden him to have them printed before having them submitted to examination by an ecclesiastical authority."[6]

It is not known in what way the Abbé Colomb used the manuscripts of his saintly confrere. In any event he did not, apparently, dream of publishing them; but he preserved them carefully, regarding them as his property. He scarcely even spoke of them, to so intimate a friend as Abbé Delaroche, his devoted collaborator in the direction of the Sisters of the Five Wounds.

The years passed. Oblivion descended upon the sermons of the Curé of Ars; nor were the famous *catechisms* remembered any better. It had got to the stage that people did not even know that there were manuscripts of the Servant of God in existence.

Perhaps they might have been ignored for the rest of time had not the identity of their custodian been quite involuntarily revealed. M. Valansio, one of the clergy of Belley, to whom the role of "Devil's Advocate" in the Cause of the Beatification of the Curé of Ars had been entrusted, took a walk one day with M. Colomb. During the course of conversation the Abbé Valansio expressed regret that no one possessed anything belonging to M. Vianney except his very few signed letters.

"But there are his sermons," replied the other.

"His sermons? . . . I would certainly like to see the color of them."

"That is easy. *I have them.*"

A few days later official notice was served upon the Abbé Colomb to hand over his manuscripts to the Bishop of Belley.

As the Abbé refused to do this Cardinal Caverot, Archbishop of Lyons, approached him in person. Again there was a refusal. The Cardinal spoke of interdict and censures. The Abbé had to give in.[7]

Towards 1880 the manuscript sermons were sent to Rome. As far back as the month of March, 1866, when appointing Cardinal Patrizzi as the Promoter of the Faith for the Cause of the Curé of Ars, Pius IX had authorized him to "designate the censors with a view to examining the writings of the pious Curé." But in Rome the copyists of the Congregation of Rites were afraid of committing errors in deciphering wrongly certain words which were written too rapidly and too nervously. The unfortunate manuscripts were sent back again to the Bishop of Belley for transcription.

Msgr. Soubiranne entrusted them to the clergy in Lyons, notably to Canon Etienne Delaroche, friend, like his brother Augustin, of the Abbé Colomb. Canon Etienne Delaroche, a doctor of theology, was archpriest of the very old church at Ainay in Lyons, while his brother Augustin had become a disciple of Dom Gréa who, in 1866, had founded at Saint Claude (Jura) the Institute of the Canons Regular of the Immaculate Conception. The French copyists did not delay; thanks to them Rome soon had the authentic and complete text of the sermons of the Curé of Ars.

In France there was also no delay in their becoming widely known. As far back as November, 1882, Etienne and Augustin Delaroche had published at the house of Vitte and Perrussel in Lyons, four volumes entitled the *Sermons of the Venerable Servant of God, Jean-Baptiste-Marie Vianney, Curé of Ars*, republished by Librairie Beauchesne, and for a long time out of print.

With regard to the original manuscripts of St. Jean-Marie-Baptiste Vianney, they are kept in Rome in the Mother House of the Canons of the Immaculate Conception (via Federico Torre, 21, Monteverde). All that escaped destruction are there with the exception of three: one which was presented, in a reliquary of crystal and gilded bronze, to [St.] Pius X in 1905; a second, which was presented in a reliquary less valuable than the first, to Cardinal Coullié, Archbishop of Lyons; a third which was preserved in the collection at Ars in a frame of gilded bronze with double crystal.

The *cahiers* of the Curé of Ars are generally made up of three or four sheets of good "handmade" linen paper, each folded in two and sewn together. Each *cahier* contains thus six to eight folios of approximately 7 by 9 or 9½ inches. The text of the sermon, in close handwriting, covers the front and the back of each sheet. A very narrow margin is kept at the left.

The paper, on the whole, is well preserved except that it is slightly soiled; but frequently the ink has run and for that reason several passages are difficult to read. Certain sermons, which must have been written during the winter, with semi-frozen ink or a hand trembling with the cold, can be read only with difficulty. However, there is no passage, it has been seen, that has remained indecipherable.

All these *cahiers* (except the three mentioned above and a fourth deposited in the archives of the Mother House of the Canons of the Immaculate Conception) have been collected together again in a casket of gilded bronze with crystal sides.

The appearance of the *Sermons of the Venerable Servant of God, Jean-Baptiste-Marie Vianney* caused a certain amount of surprise among the Catholic public and particularly among the clergy. People did not know that the *humble Curé of Ars* had left behind him a considerable quantity of oratorical work. They were even more surprised that his manuscripts, lost in the dust of half a century, had been considered worthy of being published. That M. Vianney, already proclaimed *Venerable* by the Church, had been a great saint no one doubted, but that he had been capable of writing eloquent sermons, that was quite another matter! The servant of God was the victim yet once more of that undeserved reputation for ignorance, even for stupidity, which some had given him during his lifetime.

MSGR. FRANÇOIS TROCHU

NOTES

1. Baroness de Belvey, *Apostolic Process, ne pereant, p.* 178.

2. *Guide for Pious Souls* is dedicated to the Curé of Ars. It is impossible, among the numerous prayers contained in this little volume, to distinguish those which would have been dedicated to M. Vianney. M. Peyronnet had subjected them to a few revisions. It is true that *The Delights of the Pilgrims at Ars* (Lyons 2nd Edit. 1857) contains, under the name of M. Vianney *The Blessing of Sleep* and a *Prayer to the Blessed Virgin.* Also in this are *Spiritual Reflections of the Servant of God, J.M.B. Vianney.* But how far are these reflections and prayers authentic? Two little works have been attributed to the Curé of Ars which are certainly by another hand than his: *The Guide for Pious Souls* and the *Considerations on the necessity of knowing Jesus Christ and of imitating His virtues* (Approved under his name by the Bishop of Belley (Guyot, Lyons, 1851).

3. Brother Athanasius, director of the school at Ars, *Apostolic Process in genere,* p. 204; Abbé Toccanier, assistant to M. Vianney and then his successor in the parish of Ars, *Apostolic Process ne pereant,* p. 333. Actually no one possesses a sermon on the Eucharist by M. Vianney. There are, indeed, among the manuscripts preserved in Rome, instructions on *Communion,* on the *Holy Mass,* on *Corpus Christi,* on the *Unworthy Communion,* but the pages which treat *ex professo* of the Real Presence—the best of the Saint's work perhaps—have disappeared. It is also probable that several sermons on the *Blessed Virgin* have not come down to us.

4. *Process of the Ordinary,* p. 337.

5. *Process of the Ordinary,* p. 1336-1338.

6. *Apostolic Process continuative,* p. 790.

7. According to manuscript notes of Msgr. Convert.

CONTENTS

THE SERMONS OF THE CURÉ OF ARS

"Oh how we could merit Heaven every day, my dear brethren, by doing just our ordinary duties, but by doing them for God and the salvation of our souls."

—The Curé of Ars
Page 175

"We shall never return to God if we do not have recourse to prayer. Yes, my dear children, with a prayer well said, we can command Heaven and earth, and all will obey us."

—The Curé of Ars
Page 127

"No, my dear children, we need never fear that the Mass hinders us in the fulfillment of our temporal affairs; it is altogether the other way around. We may be sure that all will go better and that even our business will succeed better than if we have the misfortune not to assist at Mass."

—The Curé of Ars
Page 147

ॐ THE DREADFUL STATE OF THE LUKEWARM SOUL

IN SPEAKING TO YOU TODAY, MY DEAR BRETHREN, OF the dreadful state of the lukewarm soul, my purpose is not to paint for you a terrifying and despairing picture of the soul which is living in mortal sin without even having the wish to escape from this condition. That poor unfortunate creature can but look forward to the wrath of God in the next life. Alas! These sinners hear me; they know well of whom I am speaking at this very moment. . . . We will go no further, for all that I would wish to say would serve only to harden them more.

In speaking to you, my brethren, of the lukewarm soul, I do not wish, either, to speak of those who make neither their Easter duty nor their annual Confession. They know very well that in spite of all their prayers and their other good works they will be lost. Let us leave them in their blindness, since they want to remain that way. . . .

Nor do I understand, brethren, by the lukewarm soul, that soul who would like to be worldly without ceasing to be a child of God. You will see such a one at one moment prostrate before God, his Savior and his Master, and the next moment similarly prostrate before the world, his idol. Poor blind creature, who gives one hand to God and the other to the world, so that he can call both to his aid, and promise his heart to each in turn! He loves God, or rather, he would like to love Him, but he would also like to please the world. Then, weary of wanting to give his allegiance to both, he ends by giving it to the world alone. This is an extraordinary life and one which offers so strange a spectacle that it is hard to persuade oneself that it could be the life of one and the same person. I am going to show you this so clearly that perhaps many among you will be hurt by it. But that will matter little to me, for I am always going to tell you what I ought to tell you, and then you will do what you wish about it. . . .

I would say further, my brethren, that whoever wants to please both the world and God leads one of the most unhappy of lives. You shall see how. Here is someone who gives himself up to the pleasures of the world or develops some evil habit. How great is his fear when he comes to fulfill his religious duties; that is, when he says his prayers, when he goes to Confession, or wants to go to Holy Communion! He does not want to be seen by those with whom he has been dancing and passing nights at the cabarets, where he has been giving himself over to many kinds of licentiousness. Has he come to the stage when he is going to deceive his confessor by hiding the worst of his actions and thus obtain permission to go to Holy Communion, or rather, to commit a sacrilege? He would prefer to go to Holy Communion before or after Mass, that is to say, when there is no one present. Yet he is quite happy to be seen by the good people who know nothing about his evil life and among whom he would like to arouse good opinions about himself. In front of devout people he talks about religion. When he is with those who have no religion, he will talk only about the pleasures of the world. He would blush to fulfill his religious practices in front of his companions or those boys and girls who share his evil ways. . . .

This is so true that one day someone asked me to allow him to go to Holy Communion in the sacristy so that no one would see him. Is it possible, my brethren, that one could think upon such horrible behavior without shuddering?

But we shall proceed further and you will see the embarrassment of these poor people who want to follow the world without—outwardly at any rate—leaving God. Here is Easter approaching. They must go to Confession. It is not, of course, that they want to go or that they feel any urge or need to receive the Sacrament of Penance. They would be only too pleased if Easter came around about once every thirty years.

But their parents still retain the exterior practice of religion. They will be happy if their children go to the altar, and they keep urging them, then, to go to Confession. In this, of course, they make a mistake. If only they would just pray for them and not torment them into committing sacrileges. So to rid themselves of the importunity of their parents, to keep up appearances, these people will get together to find out who is the best confessor to try for absolution for the first or second time.

"Look," says one, "my parents keep nagging at me because I haven't been to Confession. Where shall we go?"

"It is of no use going to our parish priest; he is too scrupulous. He would not allow us to make our Easter duty. We will have to try to find So-and-So. He let this one and that one go through, and they are worse than we are. We have done no more harm than they have."

Another will say: "I assure you that if it were not for my parents I would not make my Easter duty at all. Our catechism says that to make a good Confession we must give up sin and the occasions of sin, and we are doing neither the one nor the other. I tell you sincerely that I am really embarrassed every time Easter comes around. I will be glad when the time comes for me to settle down and to cease gallivanting. I will make a confession then of my whole life, to put right the ones I am making now. Without that I would not die happy."

"Well," another will say to him, "when that time comes you ought to go to the priest who has been hearing your confessions up to the present. He will know you best."

"Indeed no! I will go to the one who would not give me absolution, because he would not want to see me damned either."

"My word, aren't you good! That means nothing at all. They all have the same power."

"That is a good thing to remember when we are doing what we ought to do. But when we are in sin, we think otherwise. One day I went to see a girl who was pretty careless. She told me that she was not going back to Confession to the priests who were so easy and who, in making it seem as if they wanted to save you, pushed you into Hell."

That is how many of these poor blind people behave.

"Father," they will say to the priest, "I am going to Confession to you because our parish priest is too exacting. He wants to make us promise things which we cannot hold to. He would have us all saints, and that is not possible in the world. He would want us never to go to dances, nor to frequent cabarets or amusements. If someone has a bad habit, he will not give Absolution until the habit has been given up completely. If we had to do all that we should never make our Easter duty at all. My parents, who are very religious, are always after me to make my Easter duty. I will do all I can. But no one can say that he will never return to these amusements, since he never knows when he is going to encounter them."

"Ah!" says the confessor, quite deceived by this sincere-sounding talk, "I think your parish priest is perhaps a little exacting. Make your act of contrition, and I will give you Absolution. Try to be good now."

That is to say: Bow your head; you are going to trample in the adorable Blood of Jesus Christ; you are going to sell your God like Judas sold Him to His executioners, and tomorrow you will go to Holy Communion, where you will proceed to crucify Him. What horror! What abomination! Go on, vile Judas, go to the holy table, go and give death to your God and your Savior! Let your conscience cry out, only try to stifle its remorse as much as you can. . . . But I am going too far, my brethren. Let us leave these poor blind creatures in their gloom.

I think, brethren, that you would like to know what is the state of the lukewarm soul. Well, this is it. A lukewarm soul is not yet quite dead in the eyes of God because the faith, the hope, and the charity which are its spiritual life are not altogether extinct. But it is a faith without zeal, a hope without resolution, a charity without ardor. . . .

Nothing touches this soul: it hears the word of God, yes, that is true; but often it just bores it. Its possessor hears it with difficulty, more or less by habit, like someone who thinks that he knows enough about it and does enough of what he should. Any prayers which are a bit long are distasteful to him. This soul is so full of whatever it has just been doing or what it is going to do next, its boredom is so great, that this poor unfortunate thing is almost in agony. It is still alive, but it is not capable of doing anything to gain Heaven. . . .

For the last twenty years this soul has been filled with good intentions without doing anything at all to correct its habits. It is like someone who is envious of anyone who is on top of the world but who would not deign to lift a foot to try to get there himself. It would not, however, wish to renounce eternal blessings for those of the world. Yet it does not wish either to leave the world or to go to Heaven, and if it can just manage to pass its time without crosses or difficulties, it would never ask to leave this world at all. If you hear someone with such a soul say that life is long and pretty miserable, that is only when everything is not going in accordance with his desires. If God, in order to force such a soul to detach itself from temporal things, sends it any cross or suffering, it is fretful and grieving and abandons itself to grumbles and complaints and often even to a kind of despair. It seems as if it does not want to see that God has sent it these trials for its good, to detach it from this world and to draw it towards Himself. What has it done to deserve these trials? In this state a person thinks in his own mind that there are many others more blameworthy than himself who have not to submit to such trials.

In prosperous times the lukewarm soul does not go so far as to forget God, but neither does it forget itself. It knows very well how to boast about all the means it has employed to achieve its prosperity. It is quite convinced that many others would not have achieved the same success. It loves to repeat that and to hear it repeated, and every time it hears it, it is with fresh pleasure. The individual with the lukewarm soul assumes a gracious air when associating with those who flatter him. But towards those who have not paid him the respect which he believes he has deserved or who have not been grateful for his kindnesses, he maintains an air of frigid indifference and seems to indicate to them that they are ungrateful creatures who do not deserve to receive the good which he has done them. . . .

If I wanted to paint you an exact picture, my brethren, of the state of a soul which lives in tepidity, I should tell you that it is like a tortoise or a snail. It moves only by dragging itself along the ground, and one can see it getting from place to place with great difficulty. The love of God, which it feels deep down in itself, is like a tiny spark of fire hidden under a heap of ashes. The lukewarm soul comes to the point of being completely indifferent to its own loss. It has nothing left but a love without tenderness, without action, and without energy which sustains it with difficulty in all that is essential for salvation. But for all other means of Grace, it looks upon them as nothing or almost nothing. Alas, my brethren, this poor soul in its tepidity is like someone between two bouts of sleep. It would like to act, but its will has become so softened that it lacks either the force or the courage to accomplish its wishes.

It is true that a Christian who lives in tepidity still regularly —in appearance at least—fulfills his duties. He will indeed get down on his knees every morning to say his prayers. He will go to the Sacraments every year at Easter and even several times during the course of the twelve months. But in all of this there will be such a distaste, so much slackness and so much indifference, so little preparation, so little change in his way of life, that it is easy to see that he is only fulfilling his duties from habit and routine . . . because this is a feast and he is in the habit of carrying them out at such a time. His Confessions and his Communions are not sacrilegious, if you like, but they are Confessions and Communions which bear no fruit—which, far from making him more perfect and more pleasing to God, only make him more unworthy. As for his prayers, God alone knows what—without, of course, any preparation—he makes of these. In the morning it is not God who occupies his thoughts, nor the salvation of his poor soul; he is quite taken up with thoughts of work. His mind is so wrapped up in the things of earth that the thought of God has no place in it. He is thinking about what he is going to be doing during the day, where he will be sending his children and his various employees, in what way he will expedite his own work. To say his prayers, he gets down on his knees, undoubtedly, but he does not know what he wants to ask God, nor what he needs, nor even before whom he is kneeling. His careless demeanor shows this very clearly. It is a poor man indeed who, however miserable he is, wants nothing at all and loves his poverty. It is surely a desperately sick person who scorns doctors and remedies and clings to his infirmities. You can see that this lukewarm soul has no difficulty, on the slightest pretext, in talking during the course of his prayers. For no reason at all he will abandon them, partly at least, thinking that he will finish them in another moment. Does he want to offer his day to God, to say his Grace? He does all that, but often without thinking of the one who is addressed. He will not even stop working. If the possessor of the lukewarm soul is a man, he will turn his cap or his hat around in his hands as if to see whether it is good or bad, as though he had some idea of selling it. If it is a woman, she will say her prayers while slicing bread into her soup, or putting wood on the fire, or calling out to her children or maid. If you like, such distractions during prayer are not exactly deliberate. People would rather not have them, but because it is necessary to go to so much trouble and expend so much energy to get rid of them, they let them alone and allow them to come as they will.

The lukewarm Christian may not perhaps work on Sunday at tasks which seem to be forbidden to anyone who has even the slightest shred of religion, but doing some sewing, arranging something in the house, driving sheep to the fields during the times for Masses, on the pretext that there is not enough food to give them—all these things will be done without the slightest scruple, and such people will prefer to allow their souls and the souls of their employees to perish rather than endanger their animals. A man will busy himself getting out his tools and his carts and harrows and so on, for the next day; he will fill in a hole or fence a gap; he will cut various lengths of cords and ropes; he will carry out the churns and set them in order. What do you think about all this, my brethren? Is it not, alas, the simple truth? . . .

A lukewarm soul will go to Confession regularly, and even quite frequently. But what kind of Confessions are they? No preparation, no desire to correct faults, or, at the least, a desire so feeble and so small that the slightest difficulty will put a stop to it altogether. The Confessions of such a person are merely repetitions of old ones, which would be a happy state of affairs indeed if there were nothing to add to them. Twenty years ago he was accusing himself of the same things he confesses today, and if he goes to Confession for the next twenty years, he will say the same things. A lukewarm soul will not, if you like, commit the big sins. But some slander or back-biting, a lie, a feeling of hatred, of dislike, of jealousy, a slight touch of deceit or double-dealing—these count for nothing with it. If it is a woman and you do not pay her all the respect which she considers her due, she will, under the guise of pretending that God has been offended, make sure that you realize it; she could say more than that, of course, since it is she herself who has been offended. It is true that such a woman would not stop going to the Sacraments, but her dispositions are worthy of compassion. On the day when she wants to receive her God, she spends part of the morning thinking of temporal matters. If it is a man, he will be thinking about his deals and his sales. If it is a married woman, she will be thinking about her household and her children. If it is a young girl, her thoughts will be on her clothes.

If it is a boy, he will be dreaming about passing pleasures and so on. The lukewarm soul shuts God up in an obscure and ugly kind of prison. Its possessor does not crucify Him, but God can find little joy or consolation in his heart. All his dispositions proclaim that his pour soul is struggling for the breath of life. After having received Holy Communion, this person will hardly give another thought to God in all the days to follow. His manner of life tells us that he did not know the greatness of the happiness which had been his.

A lukewarm Christian thinks very little upon the state of his poor soul and almost never lets his mind run over the past. If the thought of making any effort to be better crosses his mind at all, he believes that once he has confessed his sins, he ought to be perfectly happy and at peace. He assists at Holy Mass very much as he would at any ordinary activity. He does not think at all seriously of what he is doing and finds no trouble in chatting about all sorts of things while on the way there. Possibly he will not give a single thought to the fact that he is about to participate in the greatest of all the gifts that God, all-powerful as He is, could give us. He does give some thought to the needs of his own soul, yes, but a very small and feeble amount of thought indeed. Frequently he will even present himself before the presence of God without having any idea of what he is going to ask of Him. He has few scruples in cutting out, on the least pretext, the Asperges and the prayers before Mass. During the course of the service, he does not want to go to sleep, of course, and he is even afraid that someone might see him, but he does not do himself any violence all the same. He does not want, of course, to have distractions during prayer or during the Holy Mass, yet when he should put up some little fight against them, he suffers them very patiently, considering the fact that he does not like them. Fast days are reduced to practically nothing, either by advancing the time of the main meal or, under the pretext that Heaven was never taken by famine, by making the collation so abundant that it amounts to a full meal. When he performs good or beneficial actions, his intentions are often very mixed—sometimes it is to please someone, sometimes it is out of compassion, and sometimes it is just to please the world. With such people everything that is not a really serious sin is good enough. They like doing good, being faithful, but they wish that it did not cost them anything or, at least, that it cost very little. They would like to visit the sick, indeed, but it would be more convenient if the sick would come to them. They have something to give away in alms, they know quite well that a certain person has need of help, but they wait until she comes to ask them instead of anticipating her, which would make the kindness so very much more meritorious. We will even say, my brethren, that the person who leads a lukewarm life does not fail to do plenty of good works, to frequent the Sacraments, to assist regularly at all church services, but in all of this one sees only a weak, languishing faith, hope which the slightest trial will upset, a love of God and of neighbor which is without warmth or pleasure. Everything that such a person does is not entirely lost, but it is very nearly so.

See, before God, my brethren, on what side you are. On the side of the sinners, who have abandoned everything and plunge themselves into sin without remorse? On the side of the just souls, who seek but God alone? Or are you of the number of these slack, tepid, and indifferent souls such as we have just been depicting for you? Down which road are you traveling? Who can dare assure himself that he is neither a great sinner nor a tepid soul but that he is one of the elect? Alas, my brethren, how many seem to be good Christians in the eyes of the world who are really tepid souls in the eyes of God, Who knows our inmost hearts. . . .

Let us ask God with all our hearts, if we are in this state, to give us the grace to get out of it, so that we may take the route that all the saints have taken and arrive at the happiness that they are enjoying. That is what I desire for you. . . .

६ॐ *HAVE YOU RELIGION IN YOUR HEART?*

ALAS, MY DEAR BRETHREN, WHAT HAVE WE BE-
come even since our conversion? Instead of going always forward and increasing in holiness, what laziness and what indifference we display! God cannot endure this perpetual incon-
stancy with which we pass from virtue to vice and from vice to
virtue. Tell me, my children, is not this the very pattern of the
way you live? Are your poor lives anything other than a succession of good deeds and bad deeds? Is it not true that you go
to Confession and the very next day you fall again—or perhaps
the very same day? ... How can this be, unless the religion you
have is unreal, a religion of habit, a religion of long-standing
custom, and not a religion rooted in the heart? Carry on, my
friend; you are only a waverer! Carry on, my poor man; in
everything you do, you are just a hypocrite and nothing else!
God has not the first place in your heart; that is reserved for
the world and the devil. How many people there are, my dear
children, who seem to love God in real earnest for a little while
and then abandon Him! What do you find, then, so hard and
so unpleasant in the service of God that it has repelled you so
strangely and caused you to change over to the side of the
world? Yet at the time when God showed you the state of your
soul, you actually wept for it and realized how much you had
been mistaken in your lives. If you have persevered so little,
the reason for this misfortune is that the devil must have been
greatly grieved to have lost you because he has done so much
to get you back. He hopes now to keep you altogether. How
many apostates there are, indeed, who have renounced their
religion and who are Christians in name only!

But, you will say to me, how can we know that we have religion in our hearts, this religion which is consistent?

My dear brethren, this is how: listen well and you will understand if you have religion as God wants you to have it in order to lead you to Heaven. If a person has true virtue, nothing whatever can change him; he is like a rock in the midst of a tempestuous sea. If anyone scorns you, or calumniates you, if someone mocks at you or calls you a hypocrite or a sanctimonious fraud, none of this will have the least effect upon your peace of soul. You will love him just as much as you loved him when he was saying good things about you. You will not fail to do him a good turn and to help him, even if he speaks badly of your assistance. You will say your prayers, go to Confession, to Holy Communion, you will go to Mass, all according to your general custom.

To help you to understand this better, I will give you an example. It is related that in a certain parish there was a young man who was a model of virtue. He went to Mass almost every day and to Holy Communion often. It happened that another was jealous of the esteem in which this young man was held, and one day, when they were both in the company of a neighbor, who possessed a lovely gold snuffbox, the jealous one took it from its owner's pocket and placed it, unobserved, in the pocket of the young man. After he had done this, without pretending anything, he asked to see the snuffbox. The owner expected to find it in his pocket and was astonished when he discovered that it was missing. No one was allowed to leave the room until everyone had been searched, and the snuffbox was found, of course, on the young man who was a model of goodness. Naturally, everyone immediately called him a thief and attacked his religious professions, denouncing him as a hypocrite and a sanctimonious fraud. He could not defend himself, since the box had been found in his pocket. He said nothing. He suffered it all as something which had come from the hand of

God. When he was walking along the street, when he was coming from the church, or from Mass or Holy Communion, everyone who saw him jeered at him and called him a hypocrite, a fraud, a thief. This went on for quite a long time, but in spite of it, he continued with all of his religious exercises, his Confessions, his Communions, and all of his prayers, just as if everyone were treating him with the utmost respect. After some years, the man who had been the cause of it all fell ill. To those who were with him he confessed that he had been the origin of all the evil things which had been said about this young man, who was a saint, and that through jealousy of him, so that he might destroy his good name, he himself had put the snuffbox in the young man's pocket.

There, my brethren, is a religion which is true, which has taken root in the soul. Tell me, if all of those poor Christians who make profession of religion were subjected to such trials, would they imitate this young man? Ah, my dear brethren, what murmurings there would be, what bitternesses, what thoughts of revenge, of slander, of calumny, even perhaps of going to law. . . . They would storm against religion; they would scorn and jeer at it and say nothing but ill of it; they would not be able to say their prayers any more; they would not be able to go to Mass; they would not know what more to do or to say to justify themselves; they would collect every item of harm that this or that person had done, tell it to others, repeat it to everyone who knew them in order to make them out as liars and calumniators. What is the reason for this conduct, my dear brethren? Surely it is that our religion is only one of whim, of long-standing habit and routine, and, if we were to put it more forcefully, because we are hypocrites who serve God just as long as everything is going according to our wishes. Alas, my dear brethren, all of these virtues which we observe in a great many apparent Christians are but like the flowers of spring, which one gust of hot wind can wither.

?? *LOST WORKS*

How is it, my dear brethren, that so few Christians behave with one end only in view—to please God? Here is the reason, pure and simple. It is just that the vast majority of Christians are enveloped in the most shocking ignorance, so that, humanly speaking, they really do the very best they can. The result is that if you were to compare their intentions with those of pagans, you would not find any difference. Ah, dear Lord, how many good works are lost for Heaven! Others who are a little better informed are interested only in the esteem of their fellow men, and they try to dissemble as much as they can: their exterior seems good, while interiorly they are filled with duplicity and evil. Yes, my dear brethren, we shall see at the Judgment that the largest section of Christians practiced a religion of whim or caprice only—that is to say, the greatest number of them practiced their religion merely from motives of routine, and very few sought God alone in what they did.

?? *WE ARE WRETCHED CREATURES*

We cannot dwell upon the conduct of the Jews, my dear people, without being struck with amazement. These very people had waited for God for four thousand years, they had prayed much because of the great desire they had to receive Him, and yet when He came, He could not find a single person to give Him the poorest lodging. The all-powerful God was obliged to make His dwelling with the animals. And yet, my dear people, I find in the conduct of the Jews, criminal as it was, not a subject for explanations, but a theme for the condemnation of the conduct of the majority of Christians. We can see that the Jews had formed an idea of their Redeemer which did not conform with the state of austerity in which He appeared. It seemed as if they could not persuade themselves that this could indeed be He who was to be their Savior; St. Paul tells us very clearly that if the Jews had recognized Him as God, they would never have put Him to death. There is, then, some small excuse for the Jews. But what excuse can we make, my dear brethren, for the coldness and the contempt which we show towards Jesus Christ? Oh, yes, we do indeed truly believe that Jesus Christ came upon earth, that He provided the most convincing proofs of His divinity. Hence the reason for our hope. We rejoice, and we have good reason to recognize Jesus Christ as our God, our Savior, and our Model. Here is the foundation of our faith. But, tell me, with all this, what homage do we really pay Him? Do we do more for Him than if we did not believe all this? Tell me, dear brethren, does our conduct correspond at all to our beliefs? We are wretched creatures. We are even more blameworthy than the Jews.

ℰ ROUTINE FOLLOWERS

AH, DEAR LORD, WHAT BLINDNESS! OH, UGLY SIN OF hypocrisy which leads souls to hell with actions which, if they had been performed from genuine motives, would have brought them to Heaven! Unfortunately, such a large body of Christians do not know themselves and do not even try to know themselves. They follow routines and habits, and they do not want to see reason. They are blind, and they move along in their blindness. If a priest wants to tell them about the state they are in, they do not listen, and if they go through the pretense of listening, they will do nothing at all about what they are told. This state, my dear people, is the most unhappy state that anyone can possibly imagine, and it is perhaps the most dangerous one as well.

ࣸ *THE WORLD IS EVERYTHING—GOD, NOTHING!*

IF PEOPLE WOULD DO FOR GOD WHAT THEY DO FOR the world, my dear people, what a great number of Christians would go to Heaven! But if you, dear children, had to pass three or four hours praying in a church, as you pass them at a dance or in a cabaret, how heavily the time would press upon you! If you had to go to a great many different places in order to hear a sermon, as you go for your pastimes or to satisfy your avarice and greed, what pretexts there would be, and how many detours would be taken to avoid going at all. But nothing is too much trouble when done for the world. What is more, people are not afraid of losing either God or their souls or Heaven. With what good reason did Jesus Christ, my dear people, say that the children of this world are more zealous in serving their master, the world, than the children of light are in serving theirs, who is God. To our shame, we must admit that people fear neither expense, nor even going into debt, when it is a matter of satisfying their pleasures, but if some poor person asks them for help, they have nothing at all. This is true of so many: they have everything for the world and nothing at all for God because to them, the world is everything and God is nothing.

ࣸ *FOLLOW ONE MASTER ONLY*

WHAT A SAD LIFE DOES HE LEAD WHO WANTS BOTH to please the world and to serve God! It is a great mistake to make, my friends. Apart from the fact that you are going to be unhappy all the time, you can never attain the stage at which you will be able to please the world and please God. It is as impossible a feat as trying to put an end to eternity. Take the advice that I am going to give you now and you will be less unhappy: give yourselves wholly to God or else wholly to the world. Do not look for and do not serve more than one master, and once you have chosen the one you are going to follow, do not leave him. You surely remember what Jesus Christ said to you in the Gospel: you cannot serve God and Mammon; that is to say, you cannot follow the world and the pleasures of the world and Jesus Christ with His Cross. Of course you would be quite willing to follow God just so far and the world just so far! Let me put it even more clearly: you would like it if your conscience, if your heart, would allow you to go to the altar in the morning and the dance in the evening; to spend part of the day in church and the remainder in the cabarets or other places of amusement; to talk of God at one moment and the next to tell obscene stories or utter calumnies about your neighbor; to do a good turn for your next-door neighbor on one occasion and on some other to do him harm; in other words, to do good and speak well when you are with good people and to do wrong when you are in bad company.

ঠ&ও THEY ARE FOR THE WORLD

ONE SECTION, AND PERHAPS IT IS THE LARGEST SECtion, of people everywhere are wholly wrapped up in the things of this world. And of this large number there are those who are content to have suppressed all feeling of religion, all thought of another life, who have done everything in their power to efface the terrible thought of the judgment which one day they will have to undergo. They employ all their wiles, and often their wealth, during the course of their lives to attract to their way of life as many people as they can. They no longer believe in anything. They even take a pride in making themselves out to be more impious and incredulous than they really are in order to convince others and to make them believe, not in the verities, but in the falsehoods which they wish to take root in the hearts of those under their influence.

Voltaire, in the course of a dinner given one day for his friends—that is, for the impious—rejoiced that of all those present, there was not one who believed in religion. And yet he himself did believe, as he was to show at the hour of his death. Then he demanded with great earnestness that a priest should be brought to him that he might make his peace with God. But it was too late. God, against whom he had fought and spoken with such fury all his life, dealt with him as He had with Antiochus: He abandoned him to the fury of the devils. At that dread moment, Voltaire had only despair and the thought of eternal damnation as his lot. The Holy Ghost tells us: "The fool hath said in his heart: There is no God." But it is only the corruption of his heart which could carry man to such an excess; he does not believe it in the depths of his soul. The words "There is a God" will never entirely disappear. The greatest sinner will often utter them without even thinking of what he is saying. But let us leave these blasphemous people aside. Happily, though you may not be as good Christians as you ought to be, thanks be to God you are not of that company.

But, you will say to me, who are these people who are partly on God's side and partly on the side of the world? Well, my dear children, let me describe them. I will compare them (if I may dare to make use of the term) to dogs who will run to the first person who calls them. You may follow them from the morning to the evening, from the beginning of the year to the end. These people look upon Sunday as merely a day for rest and amusement. They stay in bed longer than on weekdays, and instead of giving themselves to God with all their hearts, they do not even think of Him. Some of them will be thinking of their amusements, others of people they expect to meet, still others of the sales they are about to make or the money they will be spending or receiving. With great difficulty they will manage the Sign of the Cross in some fashion or another. Because they will be going to church later, they will omit their prayers altogether, saying: "Oh, I'll have plenty of time to say them before Mass." They always have something to do before setting out for Mass, and although they have been planning to say their prayers before setting out, they are barely in time for the beginning of the Mass itself. If they meet a friend along the road, it is no trouble to them to bring him back home and put off the Mass until a later hour.

But since they still want to appear Christian, they will go to Mass sometime later, though it will be with infinite boredom and reluctance. The thought in their minds will be: "Oh, Lord, will this ever be over!" You will see them in church, especially during the instruction, looking around from one side to the other, asking the person next to them for the time, and so on. More of them yawn and stretch and turn the pages of their prayer book as if they were examining it in order to see whether the printer had made any mistakes. There are others, and you can see them sleeping as soundly as if they were in a comfortable bed. The first thought that comes to them when they awake is not that they have been profaning so holy a place but: "Oh, Lord, this will never be over. . . . I'm not coming back any more." And finally there are those to whom the word of God (which has converted so many sinners) is actually nauseating. They are obliged to go out, they say, to get a breath of air or else they would die. You will see them, distressed and miserable, during the services. But no sooner is the service over (and often even before the priest has actually left the altar) than they will be pressing around the door from which the first of the congregation are streaming out, and you will notice that all the joy which they had lost during the service has come back again. They are so tired that often they have not the "strength" to come back to the evening service. If you were to ask them why they were not coming to this, they would tell you: "Ah, we would have to be all the day in the church. We have other things to do."

For such people there is no question of instruction, nor of the Rosary, nor of evening prayers. They look upon all these things as of no consequence. If you asked them what had been said during the instruction, they would say: "He did too much shouting. . . . He bored us to death. . . . I can't remember anything else about it. . . . If it hadn't been so long, it might have been easier to remember some of it. . . . That is just what keeps the world away from religious services—they are too long." It is quite right to say "the world" because these people belong to the camp of "the worldly," although they do not know it. But now we shall try to make them understand things a little better (at least if they want to). But, being deaf and blind (as they are), it is very difficult to make them understand the words of life or to comprehend their own unhappy state. To begin with, they never make the Sign of the Cross before a meal or say Grace afterwards, nor do they recite the Angelus. If, as a result of some old habit or training, they still observe these practices and you should happen to see the manner in which they carry them out, you would feel sick: the women will simultaneously be getting on with their work or calling to their children or members of the household; the men will be turning a hat or a cap around in their hands as if searching for holes. They think as much about God as if they really believed that He did not exist at all and that they were doing all this for a joke. They have no scruples about buying or selling on the holy day of Sunday, even though they know, or at least they should know, that dealing on a reasonably big scale on a Sunday, when there is no necessity for it, is a mortal sin. Such people regard all such facts as trifles. They will go into a parish on a holy day to hire laborers, and if you told them they were doing wrong, they would reply: "We must go when we can find them there." They have no problem, either, about paying their taxes on a Sunday because during the week they might have to go a little further and take a few moments longer to complete the job.

"Ah," you will say to me, "we wouldn't think much of all that." You would not think much of all that, my dear people, and I am not at all surprised, because you are worldly. You would like to be followers of God and at the same time to satisfy the standards of the world. Do you realize, my children, who these people are? They are the people who have not entirely lost the faith and to whom there still remains some attachment to the service of God, the people who do not want to give up all religious practices, for indeed, they themselves find fault with those who do not go often to the services, but they have not enough courage to break with the world and to turn to God's side. They do not wish to be damned, but neither do they wish to inconvenience themselves too much. They hope that they will be saved without having to do too much violence to themselves. They have the idea that God, being so good, did not create them for perdition and that He will pardon them in spite of everything; that the time will come when they will turn over to God; that they will correct their faults and abandon all their bad habits. If, in moments of reflection, they pass their petty lives before their eyes, they will lament for their faults, and sometimes they will even weep for them. . . .

What a very tragic life such people lead, my children, who want to follow the ways of the world without ceasing to be the children of God. Let us go on a little further and you will be able to understand this a little more clearly and to see for yourselves how stupid indeed such a life can be. At one moment you will hear the people who lead it praying or making an act of contrition, and the next moment you will hear them, if something is not going the way they want it, swearing or maybe even using the holy name of God. This morning you may have seen them at Mass, singing or listening to the praises of God, and on the very same day you will hear them giving vent to the most scandalous utterances. They will dip their hands in holy water and ask God to purify them from their sins; a little later they will be using those very hands in an impure way upon themselves or upon others. The same eyes which this morning had the great happiness of contemplating Jesus Christ in the Blessed Sacrament will in the course of the day voluntarily rest with pleasure upon the most immodest objects. Yesterday you saw a certain man doing an act of charity or a service for a neighbor; today he will be doing his best to cheat that neighbor if he can profit thereby. A moment ago this mother desired all sorts of blessings for her children, and now, because they are annoying her, she will shower all sorts of curses upon them: she wishes she might never see them again, that she was miles away from them, and ends up by consigning them to the Devil to rid herself of them! At one moment she sends her children to Mass or Confession; at another, she will be sending them to the dance or, at least, she will pretend not to know that they are there or forbid them to go with a laugh which is tantamount to permission to go. At one time she will be telling her daughter to be reserved and not to mix with bad companions, and at another she will allow her to pass whole hours with young men without saying a word. It's no use, my poor mother, you are on the side of the world! You think yourself to be on God's side by reason of some exterior show of religion which you make. You are mistaken; you belong to that number of whom Jesus Christ has said: "Woe to the world. . . ."

You see these people who think they are following God but who are really living up to the maxims of the world. They have no scruples about taking from their neighbor wood or fruit or a thousand and one other things. Whenever they are flattered for what they do for religion, they derive quite a lot of pleasure from their actions. They will be quite keen then and will be delighted to give good advice to others. But let them be subjected to any contempt or calumny and you will see them become discouraged and distressed because they have been treated in this way. Yesterday they wanted only to do good to anyone who did them harm, but today they can hardly tolerate such people, and often they cannot even endure to see them or to speak to them.

Poor worldlings! How unhappy you are! Go on with your daily round; you have nothing to hope for but Hell! Some would like to go to the Sacraments at least once a year, but for that, it is necessary to find an easygoing confessor. They would like . . . if only—and there is the whole problem. If they find a confessor who sees that their dispositions are not good and he refuses them Absolution, you will then find them thundering against him, justifying themselves for all they are worth for having tried and failed to obtain the Sacrament. They will speak evil about him. They know very well why they have been refused and left in their sinful state, but, as they know, too, the confessor can do nothing to grant them what they want, so they get satisfaction by saying anything they wish.

Carry on, children of this world, carry on with your daily round; you will see a day you never wished to see! It would seem then that we must divide our hearts in two! But no, my friends, that is not the case; all for God or all for the world. You would like to frequent the Sacraments? Very well, then, give up the dances and the cabarets and the unseemly amusements. Today you have sufficient grace to come here and present yourselves at the tribunal of Penance, to kneel before the Holy Table, to partake of the Bread of the Angels. In three or four weeks, maybe less, you will be seen passing your night among drunken men, and what is more, you will be seen indulging in the most horrible acts of impurity. Carry on, children of this world; you will soon be in Hell! They will teach you there what you should have done to get to Heaven, which you have lost entirely through your own fault. . . .

Woe betide you, children of this world! Carry on; follow your master as you have done up to the present! Very soon you will see clearly that you have been mistaken in following his ways. But will that make you any wiser? No, my children, it will not. If someone cheats us once, we say: "We will not trust him any more—and with good reason." The world cheats us continually and yet we love it. "Love not the world, nor the things which are in the world," St. John warns us. Ah, my dear children, if we gave some thought to what the world really is, we should pass all our lives in bidding it farewell. When one reaches the age of fifteen years, one has said farewell to the pastimes of childhood; one has come to look upon them as trifling and ephemeral, as one would the actions of children building houses of cards or sand castles. At thirty, one has begun to put behind one the consuming pleasures of passionate youth. What gave such intense pleasure in younger days is already beginning to weary. Let us go further, my dear children, and say that every day we are bidding farewell to the world. We are like travelers who enjoy the beauty of the countryside through which they are passing. No sooner do they see it than it is time for them to leave it behind. It is exactly the same with the pleasures and the good things to which we become so attached. Then we arrive at the edge of eternity, which engulfs all these things in its abyss.

It is then, my dear brethren, that the world will disappear forever from our eyes and that we shall recognize our folly in having been so attached to it. And all that has been said to us about sin! . . . Then we shall say: It was all true. Alas, I lived only for the world, I sought nothing but the world in all I did, and now the pleasures and the joys of the world are not for me any longer! They are all slipping away from me—this world which I have loved so well, these joys, these pleasures which have so fully occupied my heart and my soul! . . .

Now I must return to my God! . . . How consoling this thought is, my dear children, for him who has sought only God throughout his life! But what a despairing thought for him who has lost sight of God and of the salvation of his soul!

❧ WE ARE EXTRAORDINARILY BLIND

WE MUST CERTAINLY BE EXTRAORDINARILY BLIND because when all is said and done, there is not a single person who could say that he is ready to appear before Jesus Christ. Yet in spite of the fact that we are quite aware of this, there is still not one among us who will take a single step nearer to God. Dear Lord, how blind the sinner is! How pitiable is his lot! My dear children, let us not live like fools any longer, for at the moment when we least expect it, Jesus Christ will knock at our door. How happy then will be the person who has not been waiting until that very moment to prepare himself for Him. That is what I wish you to be.

❧ NOT LIKE THE OTHERS

I AM NOT LIKE THE OTHERS! That, my dear brethren, is the usual tone of false virtue and the attitude of those proud people who, always quite satisfied with themselves, are at all times ready to censure and to criticize the conduct of others. That, too, is the attitude of the rich, who look upon the poor as if they were of a different race or nature from them and who behave towards them accordingly. Let us go one better, my dear brethren, and admit that it is the attitude of most of the world. There are very few people, even in the lowliest conditions, who do not have a good opinion of themselves. They regard themselves as far superior to their equals, and their detestable pride urges them to believe that they are indeed worth a great deal more than most other people. From this I conclude that pride is the source of all the vices and the cause of all the evils which have occurred, and which are still to come, in the course of the centuries. We carry our blindness so far that often we even glorify ourselves on account of things which really ought to cover us with confusion. Some derive a great deal of pride because they believe that they have more intelligence than others; others because they have a few more inches of land or some money, when in fact they should be in dread of the formidable account which God will demand of them one day. Oh, my dear brethren, if only some of them felt the need to say the prayer that St. Augustine addressed to God: "My God, teach me to know myself for what I am and I shall have no need of anything else to cover me with confusion and scorn for myself."

We could say that this sin is found everywhere, that it accompanies man in what he does and says. It is like a kind of seasoning or flavoring which can be tasted in every portion of a dish. Listen to me for a moment and you can see this for yourselves. Our Lord gives us an example in the Gospel when He tells us of the Pharisee who went up into the temple to pray and, standing up where all could see him, said in a loud voice: "O God, I give thee thanks that I am not as the rest of men steeped in sin. I spend my life doing good and pleasing you." Herein consists the very nature of the proud man: instead of thanking God for condescending to make use of him for a good purpose and for giving him grace, he looks upon whatever good he does as something which comes from himself, not from God. Let us go into a few details and you will see that there are hardly any exceptions to this general sin of pride. The old and the young, the rich and the poor, all suffer from it. Each and everyone congratulates himself and flatters himself because of what he is or of what he does—or rather because of what he is not and what he does not. Everyone applauds himself and loves also to be applauded. Everyone rushes to solicit the praises of the rest of the world, and everyone strives to draw them to himself. In this way are the lives of the great majority of people passed.

The door by which pride enters with the greatest ease and strength is the door of wealth. Just as soon as someone improves his possessions and his sources of wealth, you will observe him change his mode of life. He will act as Jesus Christ told us the Pharisees liked to act: these people love to be called master and to have people saluting them. They like the first places. They begin to appear in better clothes. They leave behind their air of simplicity. If you salute them, they will, with difficulty, nod to you without raising their hats. Walking with their heads in the air, they will study to find the finest words for everything, though quite often they do not even know the meaning of the words, and they love to repeat them. In order to show that his wealth has been increased, this man will make your head swim with stories of the legacies he is going to receive. Others are preoccupied with their labors to become highly esteemed and praised. If one of them has succeeded in some undertaking, he will rush to make it known as widely as possible so that his would-be wisdom and cleverness may be spread far and wide. If another has said something which has gained approval or interest, he will deafen everyone he knows with repetition of it, until they are bored to death and make fun of him. If such vain and boastful people do any traveling at all, you will hear them exaggerating a hundred times all that they said and did to such an extent that you feel sorry for the people who have to listen to them. They think that they appear very brilliant, though people are scoffing at them in secret. No one can stop them from talking about themselves: one well-known braggart convinced himself that people believed everything he said! . . .

Observe a person of some standing scrutinizing the work of someone else. He will find a hundred faults with it and will say: "Ah, what can you expect? He does not know any better!" But since the proud person never depreciates the merit of someone else without increasing his own importance, he will hurry on then to speak of some work which he has done, which So-and-So has considered so well executed that he has talked about it to many others.

Take a young woman who has a shapely figure or who, at any rate, thinks she has. You see her walking along, picking her steps, full of affectation, with a pride which seems colossal enough to reach the clouds! If she has plenty of clothes, she will leave her wardrobe open so that they can be seen. People take pride in their animals and in their households. They take pride in knowing how to go to Confession properly, in saying their prayers, in behaving modestly and decorously in the church. A mother takes pride from her children. You will hear a landowner whose fields are in better condition than those of his neighbors criticizing these and applauding his own superior knowledge. Or it may be a young man with a watch, or perhaps only the chain, and a couple of coins in his pocket, and you will hear him saying, "I did not know that it was so late," so that people will see him looking at the watch or will know that he has one. You may observe a man gambling; he may have but two coins to spare, but he will have all he possesses in his hand, and sometimes even what is not his. Or indeed, he will even pretend that he has more than he really has. How many people even borrow, either money or clothes, just to go to places of gambling or other kinds of pleasure.

No, my dear brethren, there is nothing that is quite as ridiculous or stupid as to be forever talking about what we have or what we do. Just listen to the father of a family when his children are of an age to get married; in all the places and gatherings where he is to be found you will hear him saying:

"I have so many thousand francs ready; my business will give me so many thousands, etc."

But if later he is asked for a few coppers for the poor, he has nothing.

If a tailor or a dressmaker has made a success of a coat or a frock and someone seeing the wearer pass says, "That looks very well. I wonder who made it?" they will make very sure to observe: "Oh, I made that."

Why? So that everyone may know how skillful they are.

But if the garment had not been such a success, they would, of course, take good care to say nothing, for fear of being humiliated. The housewives in their own domain . . .[1]

And I will add this to what I have just said. This sin is even more to be feared in people who put on a good show of piety and religion.

₹❧ *THE EVIL TONGUES*

THERE ARE SOME WHO, THROUGH ENVY, FOR THAT is what it amounts to, belittle and slander others, especially those in the same business or profession as their own, in order to draw business to themselves. They will say such evil things as "their merchandise is worthless" or "they cheat"; that they have nothing at home and that it would be impossible to give goods away at such a price; that there have been many complaints about these goods; that they will give no value or wear or whatever it is, or even that it is short weight, or not the right length, and so on. A workman will say that another man is not a good worker, that he is always changing his job, that people are not satisfied with him, or that he does no work, that he only puts in his time, or perhaps that he does not know how to work.

"What I was telling you there," they will then add, "it would be better to say nothing about it. He might lose by it, you know."

"Is that so?" you answer. "It would have been better if you yourself had said nothing. That would have been the thing to do."

A farmer will observe that his neighbor's property is doing better than his own. This makes him very angry so he will speak evil of him. There are others who slander their neighbors from motives of vengeance. If you do or say something to help someone, even through reasons of duty or of charity, they will then

[1] Sentence incomplete.—Trans.

look for opportunities to decry you, to think up things which will harm you, in order to revenge themselves. If their neighbor is well spoken of, they will be very annoyed and will tell you:

"He is just like everyone else. He has his own faults. He has done this, he has said that. You didn't know that? Ah, that is because you have never had anything to do with him."

A great many people slander others because of pride. They think that by depreciating others they will increase their own worth. They want to make the most of their own alleged good qualities. Everything they say and do will be good, and everything that others say and do will be wrong.

But the great bulk of malicious talk is done by people who are simply irresponsible, who have an itch to chatter about others without feeling any need to discover whether what they are saying is true or false. They just have to talk. Yet, although these latter are less guilty than the others—that is to say, than those who slander and backbite through hatred or envy or revenge—yet they are not free from sin. Whatever the motive that prompts them, they should not sully the reputation of their neighbor.

It is my belief that the sin of scandalmongering includes all that is most evil and wicked. Yes, my dear brethren, this sin includes the poison of all the vices—the meanness of vanity, the venom of jealousy, the bitterness of anger, the malice of hatred, and the flightiness and irresponsibility so unworthy of a Christian. . . . Is it not, in fact, scandalmongering which sows almost all discord and disunity, which breaks up friendships and hinders enemies from reconciling their quarrels, which disturbs the peace of homes, which turns brother against brother, husband against wife, daughter-in-law against mother-in-law and son-in-law against father-in-law? How many united households have been turned upside down by one evil tongue, so that their members could not bear to see or to speak to one another? And one malicious tongue, belonging to a neighbor, man or woman, can be the cause of all this misery. . . .

Yes, my dear brethren, the evil tongue of one scandalmonger poisons all the virtues and engenders all the vices. It is from that malicious tongue that a stain is spread so many times through a whole family, a stain which passes from fathers to children, from one generation to the next, and which perhaps is never effaced. The malicious tongue will follow the dead into the grave; it will disturb the remains of these unfortunates by making live again the faults which were buried with them in that resting place. What a foul crime, my dear brethren! Would you not be filled with fiery indignation if you were to see some vindictive wretch rounding upon a corpse and tearing it into a thousand pieces? Such a sight would make you cry out in horror and compassion. And yet the crime of continuing to talk of the faults of the dead is much greater. A great many people habitually speak of someone who has died something after this fashion:

"Ah, he did very well in his time! He was a seasoned drinker. He was as cute as a fox. He was no better than he should have been."

But perhaps, my friend, you are mistaken, and although everything may have been exactly as you have said, perhaps he is already in Heaven, perhaps God has pardoned him. But, in the meantime, where is your charity?

ह्ल *A PUBLIC PLAGUE*

As you know, my dear brethren, we are bound as fellow creatures to have human sympathy and feelings for one another. Yet one envious person would like, if he possibly could, to destroy everything good and profitable belonging to his neighbor. You know, too, that as Christians we must have boundless charity for our fellow men. But the envious person is far removed indeed from such virtues. He would be happy to see his fellow man ruin himself. Every mark of God's generosity towards his neighbor is like a knife thrust that pierces his heart and causes him to die in secret. Since we are all members of the same Body of which Jesus Christ is the Head, we should so strive that unity, charity, love, and zeal can be seen in one and all. To make us all happy, we should rejoice, as St. Paul tells, in the happiness of our fellow men and mourn with those who have cares or troubles. But, very far from experiencing such feelings, the envious are forever uttering scandals and calumnies against their neighbors. It appears to them that in this way they can do something to assuage and sweeten their vexation.

But, unfortunately, we have not said all that can be said about envy. This is the deadly vice which hurls kings and emperors from their thrones. Why do you think, my dear brethren, that among these kings, these emperors, these men who occupy the first places in the world of men, some are driven out of their places of privilege, some are poisoned, others are stabbed? It is simply because someone wants to rule in their place. It is not the food, nor the drink, nor the habitations that the authors of such crimes want. Not at all. They are consumed with envy.

Take another example. Here is a merchant who wants to have all the business for himself and to leave nothing at all for anyone else. If someone leaves his store to go elsewhere, he will do his best to say all the evil he can, either about the rival businessman himself or else about the quality of what he sells. He will take all possible means to ruin his rival's reputation, saying that the other's goods are not of the same quality as his own or that the other man gives short weight. You will notice, too, than an envious man like this has a diabolical trick to add to all this: "It would not do," he will tell you, "for you to say this to anyone else; it might do harm and that would upset me very much. I am only telling you because I would not like to see you being cheated."

A workman may discover that someone else is now going to work in a house where previously he was always employed. This angers him greatly, and he will do everything in his power to run down this "interloper" so that he will not be employed there after all.

Look at the father of a family and see how angry he becomes if his next-door neighbor prospers more than he or if the neighbor's land produces more. Look at a mother: she would like it if people spoke well of no children except hers. If anyone praises the children of some other family to her and does not say something good of hers, she will reply, "They are not perfect," and she will become quite upset. How foolish you are, poor mother! The praise given to others will take nothing from your children.

Just look at the jealousy of a husband in respect of his wife or of a wife in respect of her husband. Notice how they inquire into everything the other does and says, how they observe everyone to whom the other speaks, every house into which the other enters. If one notices the other speaking to someone, there will be accusations of all sorts of wrongdoing, even though the whole episode may have been completely innocent.

This is surely a cursed sin which puts a barrier between brothers and sisters, too. The very moment that a father or a mother gives more to one member of the family than the others, you will see the birth of this jealous hatred against the parent or against the favored brother or sister—a hatred which may last for years, and sometimes even for a lifetime. There are children who keep a watchful eye upon their parents just to insure that they will not give any sort of gift or privilege to one member of the family. If this should occur in spite of them, there is nothing bad enough that they will not say.

We can see that this sin makes its first appearance among children. You will notice the petty jealousies they will feel against one another if they observe any preferences on the part of the parents. A young man would like to be the only one considered to have intelligence, or learning, or a good character. A girl would like to be the only one who is loved, the only one well dressed, the only one sought after; if others are more popular than she, you will see her fretting and upsetting herself, even weeping, perhaps, instead of thanking God for being neglected by creatures so that she may be attached to Him alone. What a blind passion envy is, my dear brethren! Who could hope to understand it?

Unfortunately, this vice can be noted even among those in whom it should never be encountered—that is to say, among those who profess to practice their religion. They will take note of how many times such a person remains to go to Confession or of how So-and-So kneels or sits when she is saying her prayers. They will talk of these things and criticize the people concerned, for they think that such prayers or good works are done only so that they may be seen, or in other words, that they are purely an affectation. You may tire yourself out telling them that their neighbor's actions concern him alone. They are irritated and offended if the conduct of others is thought to be superior to their own.

You will see this even among the poor. If some kindly person gives a little bit extra to one of them, they will make sure to speak ill of him to their benefactor in the hope of preventing him from benefiting on any further occasion. Dear Lord, what a detestable vice this is! It attacks all that is good, spiritual as well as temporal.

We have already said that this vice indicates a mean and petty spirit. That is so true that no one will admit to feeling envy, or at least no one wants to believe that he has been attacked by it. People will employ a hundred and one devices to conceal their envy from others. If someone speaks well of another in our presence, we keep silence: we are upset and annoyed. If we must say something, we do so in the coldest and most unenthusiastic fashion. No, my dear children, there is not a particle of charity in the envious heart. St. Paul has told us that we must rejoice in the good which befalls our neighbor. Joy, my dear brethren, is what Christian charity should inspire in us for one another. But the sentiments of the envious are vastly different.

I do not believe that there is a more ugly and dangerous sin than envy because it is hidden and is often covered by the attractive mantle of virtue or of friendship. Let us go further and compare it to a lion which we thought was muzzled, to a serpent covered by a handful of leaves which will bite us without our noticing it. Envy is a public plague which spares no one.

We are leading ourselves to Hell without realizing it.

But how are we then to cure ourselves of this vice if we do not think we are guilty of it? I am quite certain that of the thousands of envious souls honestly examining their consciences, there would not be one ready to believe himself belonging to that company. It is the least recognized of sins. Some people are so profoundly ignorant that they do not recognize a quarter of their ordinary sins. And since the sin of envy is more difficult to know, it is not surprising that so few confess it and correct it. Because they are not guilty of the big public sins committed by coarse and brutalized people, they think that the sins of envy are only little defects in charity, when, in fact, for the most part, these are serious and deadly sins which they are harboring and tending in their hearts, often without fully recognizing them.

"But," you may be thinking in your own minds, "if I really recognized them, I would do my best to correct them."

If you want to be able to recognize them, my dear brethren, you must ask the Holy Ghost for His light. He alone will give you this grace. No one could, with impunity, point out these sins to you; you would not wish to agree nor to accept them; you would always find something which would convince you that you had made no mistake in thinking and acting in the way you did. Do you know yet what will help to make you know the state of your soul and to uncover this evil sin hidden in the secret recesses of your heart? It is humility. Just as pride will hide it from you, so will humility reveal it to you.

૨૭ *YOUR HEART IS BUT A MASS OF PRIDE*

YOU WILL TELL ME, PERHAPS, THAT YOU NEVER judge people except by what you see or after you have actually heard or been the witness of some action:

"I saw him doing this action, so I am sure. I heard what he said with my own ears. After that, I could not be mistaken."

But I shall reply by telling you to begin by entering into your own heart, which is but a mass of pride wherein everything is dried up. You will find yourself infinitely more guilty than the person whom you are so boldly judging, and you have plenty of room for fear, lest one day you will see him going to Heaven while you are being dragged down to Hell by the demons. "Oh, unfortunate pride," says St. Augustine to us, "you dare to judge your brother on the slightest appearance of evil, and how do you know that he has not repented of his fault and that he is not numbered among God's friends? Take care rather that he does not take the place which your pride is putting you in great danger of losing."

Yes, my dear brethren, all these rash judgments and all these interpretations come only from a person who has a secret pride, who does not know himself, and who dares to wish to know the interior life of his neighbor, something which is known to God alone. If only, my dear children, we were able to arrive at the stage of eradicating this first of the capital sins from our hearts, our neighbor would never do any wrong according to us. We should never amuse ourselves by examining his conduct. We should be content to do nothing else save weep for our own sins and work as hard as we could to correct them.

THE TONGUE OF THE SCANDAL-MONGER

ANYONE WHO IS UNFORTUNATE ENOUGH TO COME under the tongue of the scandalmonger is like a grain of corn under the grinding stone in a mill: he is torn, crushed, entirely destroyed. People like these will fasten onto you intentions that you never had; they will poison all your actions and your movements. If you have enough piety to wish to fulfill your religious duties, you are only a hypocrite, an angel in the church and a demon in the house. If you do any good or charitable works, they will think that this is just through pride and so that you may gain notice. If you are not worldly and not interested in worldly affairs, you are said to be odd and singular and to have no spirit. If you look after your own affairs carefully, you are nothing but a miser. Let me go further, my dear brethren, and say that the tongue of the scandalmonger is like the worm which gnaws at the good fruit—that is, the best actions that people do—and tries to turn all to bad account. The tongue of the scandalmonger is a grub which taints the most beautiful of the flowers and upon them leaves behind it the disgusting trace of is own slime.

OH, EVERYONE SAYS SO!

HAVE YOU EVER LISTENED TO SOMEONE SPEAKING well of a young woman and recounting her good qualities?

Someone else will certainly tell you that if this young woman has good qualities, she has plenty of bad ones, too. . . . She is frequenting the company of So-and-So, who does not have a good reputation. . . . I am very full sure they are not seeing each other for any good purpose. . . . And what about this other woman, who is always so well dressed and who keeps her children dressed up, too? . . . She would do much better to pay her debts. . . . And then there is this other one: she always seems good and pleasant to everyone, but if you knew her as well as I do, you would have a different opinion. . . . She only puts on all these smiles as a blind. . . . Such and such a man is going to ask her to marry him, but if he asked my advice, I could tell him a few things he doesn't know. . . .

"Who is that person going past?" asks someone else.

"Ah, well, if you don't know her, it's no great loss. I won't say any more about her. Keep out of her company—it's a cause of scandal. Everyone thinks so. Listen, the very worst people are ones like her who put up to be good and holy. Anyway, it's always the way that the people who want to pass for virtuous or pious are the most wicked and spiteful."

"She must have done you some grave harm. Has she?"

"Oh, no! But you know well that they are all the same. I happened to be with one of my oldest acquaintances one day, and I discovered that he was quite a heavy drinker and a real blackguard."

"Maybe he did something which angered you?" the other will say.

"Ah, no, he never said anything to me which shouldn't have been said, but everyone thinks that of him."

"If it weren't you who told me, I would never have believed it."

"When he's with people who do not know him, he knows very well how to act the hypocrite in order to make people believe that he is a very decent fellow. It's like one day I happened to be with So-and-So, whom you know very well—he is another virtuous man. If he doesn't do anyone any harm, he doesn't deserve any credit for that. It is just that he is not in a position to do so. I assure you that I would not like to find myself alone with him."

"He did you some harm sometime perhaps?"

"He did not indeed, because I have never had anything to do with him."

"And how do you know, then, that he is so bad?"

"Oh, it's not hard to find that out. Everyone says he is. He is just like that one who was with you one day—to hear him talk you would say that he is the most charitable man in the world and that he would never refuse anything to anyone who asked him for help. And all the time he would travel ten miles to gain two pennies. I assure you that nowadays you can't know people at all; you can't trust anyone. It is just the same with that fellow you were talking to just now. He looks after his affairs very well; he keeps up a good appearance always, and all his family look well turned out, too. . . . It's not so very difficult, really— he works at night, you know."

"Have you seen him taking anything, then?"

"Oh, no, I have never seen him taking anything. But I was told that one fine night he went back into his house well loaded with stuff. In any case, he has none too good a reputation."

And the speaker concludes: "I'm not saying that I have no faults myself, but I would be eternally sorry to be as worthless as some of these people."

In all of this you can see the notorious Pharisee, who fasts twice a week, who pays tithes of all he possesses, and who thanks God that he is not as the rest of men—extortioners, un- just, adulterers! Here you can see this pride, this hatred, this jealousy!

࿐ ST. NICHOLAS AND THE THREE GIRLS

TELL ME, NOW, MY BRETHREN, ON WHAT FOUNDA- tion are rash judgments and sentences based? Alas! They are based upon very slight evidence only, and most often upon what "someone said." But perhaps you are going to tell me that you have seen and heard this and that. Unfortunately, you could be mistaken in the testimony of both your sight and hearing, as you are going to see. . . . Here is an example which will show you, better than anything else can, how easily we can be mistaken and how we are nearly always wrong.

What would you have said, my dear brethren, if you had been living during the time of St. Nicholas and you had seen him coming in the middle of the night, walking around the house of three young girls, watching carefully and taking good care that no one saw him. Just look at that bishop, you would have thought at once, degrading and dishonoring his calling; he is a dreadful hypocrite. He seems to be a saint when he is in church, and look at him now, in the middle of the night, at the door of three girls who do not have a very good reputation!

And yet, my dear brethren, this bishop, who would certainly have been condemned by you, was indeed a very great saint and most dear to God. What he was doing was the best deed in the world. In order to spare these young persons the shame of begging, he came in the night and threw money in to them through their window because he feared that it was poverty which had made them abandon themselves to sin.

This should teach us never to judge the actions of our neighbor without having reflected very well beforehand. Even then, of course, we are only entitled to make such judgments if we are responsible for the behavior of the people concerned, that is, if we are parents or employers, and so on. As far as all others are concerned, we are nearly always wrong. Yes indeed, my brethren, I have seen people making wrong judgments about the intentions of their neighbor when I have known perfectly well that these intentions were good. I have tried in vain to make them understand, but it was no good. Oh! Cursed pride, what evil you do and how many souls do you lead to Hell! Answer me this, my dear brethren. Are the judgments which we make about the actions of our neighbor any better founded than those which would have been made by anyone who might have seen St. Nicholas walking around that house and trying to find the window of the room wherein were the three girls?

It is not to us that other people will have to render an account of their lives, but to God alone. But we wish to set ourselves up as judges of what does not concern us. The sins of others are for others, that is, for themselves, and our sins are our own business. God will not ask us to render an account of what others have done but solely of what we ourselves have done. Let us watch over ourselves, then, and not torment ourselves so much about others, thinking over and talking about what they have done or said. All that, my dear brethren, is just so much labor lost, and it can only arise from a pride comparable to that of the Pharisee who concerned himself solely with thinking about and misjudging his neighbor instead of occupying himself with thoughts of his own sins and weeping for his own poor efforts. Let us leave the conduct of our neighbor on one side, my dear brethren, and content ourselves with saying, like the holy King David: Lord, give me the grace to know myself as I really am, so that I may see what displeases Thee, and how to correct it, repent, and obtain pardon.

No, my dear brethren, while anyone passes his time in watching the conduct of other people, he will neither know nor belong to God.

ବ THE SEWER OF HELL

THERE IS YET ANOTHER FORM OF WRONGDOING which is all the more deplorable in that it is more common, and that is licentious talk. There is nothing more abominable, my dear brethren, nothing more horrible than such talk. Indeed, my children, what could be more out of keeping with the holiness of our religion than impure language? It outrages God, it scandalizes our neighbor. To put it even more clearly, loose talk releases all the passions. Very often it requires only one immodest or unseemly word to start a thousand evil thoughts, a thousand shameful desires, perhaps even to cause a fall into an infinite number of other sins and to bring to innocent souls evil of which they had been happily ignorant.

Can the Christian really afford to occupy his mind with such horrible images, a Christian who is the temple of the Holy Ghost, a Christian who has been sanctified by contact with the most adorable Body and precious Blood of Jesus Christ? Oh, Lord, if we had but some small idea of what we do when we commit sin! If our Lord has taught us that we may judge the tree by its fruit, you may judge after listening to the talk of certain people what must be the corruption of their hearts; and yet such corruption is very commonly encountered.

What sort of conversation do you hear among young people? Is there anything in their mouths but this kind of loose talk? Go—I dare to say it with St. John Chrysostom—go into these cabarets, into these haunts of impurity! What does the conversation turn upon, even among elderly people? Are they not trying to make a name for themselves by seeing who can be the most outrageous? Their mouths are like some sewer that Hell makes use of to spew its filth and its impurities over the earth and drag souls down to its depths. What are these bad Christians—or rather these envoys from the nether regions—doing? Instead of singing the praises of God, their songs are shameful and hideous; they are songs which ought to make a Christian die of horror. Oh, great God, who would not tremble at the thought of what God's judgment of all this will be! If, as Jesus Christ Himself tells us, not a single idle word will be unpunished, alas! What will be the punishment for these licentious conversations, these indecent topics, these shameful and horrible images, which make the hair stand on end? If you would imagine how blind these poor unhappy people are, just listen to them talking after this fashion:

"I had no bad intention," they will tell you, "it was just for a laugh; these things are only trifles, little stupid things, that mean nothing at all."

Is that so, my dear brethren? A sin so horrible in God's eyes that sacrilege alone surpasses it in evil! This is a trifle to you? No, it is your hearts which are destroyed and corrupted! No! No! No one can afford to laugh or joke about something from which we should fly in horror, as we would from some pursuing beast which wanted to devour us. Besides, my dear brethren, what a crime it is to like something which God wants us to detest with all our hearts! You may tell me that you had no bad intentions, but tell me this, too, miserable and wretched tool of Hell, what about those who are listening to you—do they have less bad thoughts and criminal desires after they have heard you? Will your harmless intention stay the workings of their imaginations and their hearts? Be honest and tell me that you are, in fact, the cause of the loss and eternal damnation of their souls! How many souls are hurled into Hell because of this sin? The Holy Ghost tells us that this ugly sin of impurity has covered the whole surface of the earth.

I will say no more now on this subject, my children. I will return to it in an instruction when I shall do my best to depict it for you again with even more horror.

&ra "A CURSE WILL FALL"

How is it that you are complaining that your animals are dying? Undoubtedly you must have forgotten all those sins which have been committed in your outhouses and stables during the five or six months of winter. You have forgotten that the Holy Ghost has said that everywhere this sin shall be committed, the curse of the Lord will fall. How many young people—alas!—would still have their innocence if they had not attended certain *winter gatherings,*[2] young people who

[2] The French word is *veillée,* which means a vigil or a night watch, or an evening spent in company. In rural France, in this latter sense, it means an evening spent socially in a neighbor's house, especially during the winter months. In the Curé's day, these could be all-night affairs, with dancing, drinking, and much more.—Trans.

now perhaps will never come back to God? Again, as a result of these affairs, there are those young people who form associations which, most frequently, end in scandal and the loss of a girl's reputation. Then there are all the young libertines, who, having sold their own souls to the Devil, now set out to rob others of theirs. Yes, my children, the evil which results from these gatherings is incalculable. If you are Christians and you wish to save your souls and those of your children and others of your household, you should never hold these gatherings in your homes, or at least not unless you yourselves, one of the heads of the household, are going to see to it that God will not be offended by what goes on. Once you have all come in, you should close the door and refuse to admit anyone else. Begin your gatherings by reciting one or two decades of the Rosary to invoke the protection of the Blessed Virgin—and this you can do if you put your mind to it. Then banish all lascivious and sinful songs; your bodies are temples of the Holy Ghost, and these profane your hearts and mouths; banish also all those stories that are only lies and yarns in any event and are most often directed against people consecrated to God, which makes them more sinful. And you should never allow your children into any other of these gatherings. Why do they want to get away from you, except for the purpose of avoiding supervision? If you are faithful to the fulfillment of your duties, God will be less offended and you less blameworthy.

ᘓ *ARE YOUR AFFAIRS GOING BETTER?*

ANOTHER BAD HABIT WHICH IS VERY COMMON IN homes and among working people is impatience, grumbling, and swearing. Now, my children, where do you get with your impatience and your grumbling? Do your affairs go any better? Do they cause you any less trouble? Is it not, rather, the other way around? You have a lot more trouble with them, and, what is even worse, you lose all the merit which you might have gained for Heaven.

But, you will tell me, that is all very well for those who have nothing to put up with. . . . If they were in my shoes they would probably be much worse. . . .

I would agree with all that, my children, if we were not Christians, if we had nothing to hope for beyond what benefits and pleasures we might taste in this world. I would agree if—I repeat—we were the first people who ever suffered anything, but since the time of Adam until the present, all the saints have had something to suffer, and most of them far more than have we. But they suffered with patience, always subject to the will of God, and soon their troubles were finished, and their happiness, which has begun, will never come to an end. Let us contemplate, my dear brethren, this beautiful Heaven, let us think about the happiness which God has prepared for us there, and we shall endure all the evils of life in a spirit of penitence, with the hope of an eternal reward. If only you could have the happiness of being able to say in the evening that your whole day had been spent for God!

I tell you that working people, if they want to get to Heaven, should endure patiently the rigor of the seasons and the ill humor of those for whom they work; they should avoid those grumbles and bad language so commonly heard and fulfill their duties conscientiously and faithfully. Husbands and wives should live peacefully in their union of marriage; they should be mutually edifying to each other, pray for one another, bear patiently with one another's faults, encourage virtue in one another by good example, and follow the holy and sacred rules of their state, remembering that they are the children of the saints and that, consequently, they ought not to behave like pagans, who have not the happiness of knowing the one true God.

Masters should take the same care of their servants as of their own children, remembering the warning of St. Paul that if they do not have care for them, they are worse than the pagans, and that they will be more severely punished on the day of judgment. Servants are to give you service and to be loyal to you, and you must treat them not as slaves but as your children and your brethren.

Servants must look upon their masters as taking the place of Jesus Christ on earth. Their duty is to serve them joyfully, obey them with a good grace, without grumbling, and look after their well-being as carefully as they would their own.

Servants should avoid the growth of too-familiar relationships, which are so dangerous and so fatal to innocence. If you have the misfortune to find yourself in such a situation, you must leave your employment, no matter what it may cost you to do so. Here is an example of those very circumstances wherein you must follow the counsel Jesus Christ gave you when He said that if one's right eye or right hand should be an occasion of sin, one must deprive oneself of them because it is better to go into Heaven lacking an eye or a hand than to be cast into Hell with one's whole body. That is to say, however desirable your position may be, you must leave it at once; otherwise you will never save your soul. Put the salvation of your soul first, our Lord Jesus Christ tells us, because that is the only thing you ought really to have at heart. Alas, my dear brethren, how rare are those Christians who are ready to suffer rather than to jeopardize the salvation of their souls!

ৡ৵ BAD COMPANY

My dear brethren, i call that man bad company who is without religion, who does not concern himself with either the commandments of God or those of the Church, who does not recognize Lent or Easter, who seldom comes to church or, if he does come, then only to scandalize others by his irreligious ways. You ought to shun his company; otherwise you will not be long in becoming like him without your even noticing it. He will teach you, with his bad talk as much as by his bad example, to despise the holiest things and to neglect your own most sacred duties. He will begin to turn your devotion into ridicule, to make some jokes about religion and its ministers. He will speak to you at length, in scandalous terms, about the priests or about Confession to such effect that he will cause you to lose entirely your taste for the frequent reception of the Sacraments. He will discuss the instructions of your pastors only in order to turn them into ridicule, and you can be quite certain that if you keep company with him for any length of time, you will see that, without even realizing it, you will begin to lose all taste for anything which is profitable towards the salvation of your soul.

I call bad company, my dear brethren, this young or this old slanderer who has nothing but bad and foul words in his mouth. Take good care, my children, for this type of person has a poison of his own! If you frequent his company, you may be quite certain that you will imbibe it and that, without a miracle of grace, you will die spiritually. The Devil will make good use of this wretch to sully your imagination and to corrupt your heart.

I would call that person bad company, my dear brethren, who is curious or restless or backbiting, who wants to know all that goes on in other people's houses, and who is always ready to form judgments about what he does not see at all. The Holy Ghosts tells us that these people are not only hateful to the whole world but are also accursed of God. Fly from them, my dear brethren; otherwise you will become like them. You yourselves will perish with them.

&~ ANGER DOES NOT TRAVEL ALONE

AH, MY DEAR LORD, WHAT MELANCHOLY COMPANY
is that person who is a slave to anger! Look at a poor wife who
has a husband like this. If she has a fear of God and wants to
prevent her husband from offending Him and treating her
badly, she cannot say a word, even when she most desires to do
so. She must content herself with weeping in secret in order not
to have quarrels in the home and risk giving scandal.

"But," an irritable husband will say to me, "why does she
contradict me? Everyone knows that I am hot tempered."

"You are hot tempered, my friend, but do you think that
others are not, just as much as you are? Say rather, then, that
you have no religion, and you will describe what you are. Are
not all who have a fear of God obliged to know how to govern
their passions instead of allowing themselves to be governed by
them?"

Alas! If I have said that there are women who are unfortunate because they have husbands who are irritable and bad tempered, there are husbands who are no less unfortunate in having
wives who do not know how to say a single gracious word,
whom nothing can interest or absorb, except themselves. And
what unhappiness results in that household where neither the
one nor the other wants to give way! There are nothing but disputes, quarrels, and recriminations. Oh, dear God, is not this a
real Hell? Alas, what training for the children of such homes!
What lessons in wisdom and sweetness of temper can they receive? St. Basil tells us that anger makes a man resemble the
Devil because it is only the Devil who is capable of giving way
to these kinds of excesses. . . . And I would add that anger never

travels alone. It is always accompanied by plenty of other sins. . . .

You have heard an angry father using bad language, uttering imprecations and curses. Very well, then. Listen to his children when they are angry—the same vile words, the same imprecations, and all the rest of it. Thus the vices of the parents—like their good qualities—pass to their children, but in more pronounced fashion. Cannibals kill only strangers, to eat them, but among Christians there are fathers and mothers who, in order to gratify their passions, desire the death of those to whom they have given life and who consign to the Devil those whom Jesus Christ redeemed with His precious Blood. How many times does one not hear those fathers and mothers who have no religion saying: "This cursed child. . . . You make me sick. . . . I wish you were miles away. . . . This so-and-so of a child. . . . These little brats. . . . This demon of a child. . . ." And so on.

Oh, dear Lord, that such ugly and evil phrases should fall from the lips of fathers and mothers who should desire nothing but benedictions from Heaven upon their poor little children. If we encounter so many children who are wild and undisciplined, without religion, bad tempered and stunted in their souls, we need not—at least in the great majority of cases—search for the cause beyond the curses and bad tempers of the parents.

What, then, must we think of the sin of those who curse themselves in moments of worry and difficulty? This is an appalling crime which is contrary to nature and to grace, for both nature and grace inspire us with love for ourselves. Those who curse themselves are like insane people who die by their own hands. It is even worse than that. Often they lay the blame upon their own souls, saying: "Let God damn me! I wish the Devil would carry me off! I'd rather be in Hell than the way I am."

Oh, miserable creature, says St. Augustine, may God not take you at your word, for if He did, you would go to vomit the poison of your spleen in Hell. Oh, Lord, if a Christian but thought of what he said. . . . How wretched indeed is the man who is the victim of anger! Will anyone ever be able to understand his mentality?

How about the sin, then, of a husband and wife, of a brother and sister, who spew out all sorts of blasphemies upon one another? They would tear out one another's eyes if they could, or even take away each other's very lives.

"So-and-so wife!" or "So-and-so husband!" they scream, "I wish I had never seen or known you. . . . My father was a fool to advise me to marry you! . . ."

What horror is this, coming from Christians who should strive only to become saints! Instead, they do only that which will make them demons and outcasts from Heaven! How often have we not seen brothers and sisters wishing death to one another, swearing at one another, because one is richer than the other or because of some wrong they have received? We see them nursing hatred all their lives long and even finding great difficulty in forgiving one another in the face of death.

It is just as great a sin to curse the weather, animals, or work. Just listen to all the people when the weather is not to their liking, swearing at it and exclaiming: "So-and-so weather, are you never going to change!"

They do not appreciate what they are saying. It is as if they were to say: "Oh, so-and-so God, who will not give me the weather that I want!"

Others swear at their animals: "You so-and-so beast, I can't make you go as I want you to. . . . May the Devil carry you off! . . . I hope a thunderbolt will fall on you! . . . May the fire of Heaven roast you! . . .

Alas! Unhappy, bad-tempered people, your curses take effect more often than you think. . . .

But what should we do then? This is what we should do. We should make use of all the annoyances that happen to us to remind ourselves that since we are in revolt against God, it is but just that other creatures should revolt against us. We should never give others occasion to curse us. . . . If something irritating or troublesome happens, instead of loading with curses whatever is not going the way we want it to, it would be just as easy and a great deal more beneficial for us to say: "God bless it!"

Imitate the holy man Job, who blessed the name of the Lord in all the troubles which befell him, and you will receive the same graces as he did. . . . This is what I desire for you.

৯ HOW DEATH WILL REVEAL THIEVES!

I DO NOT WISH TO SPEAK TO YOU, MY DEAR BRETHren, about those who lend at seven, eight, nine, and ten per cent. Let us leave such people to one side. To make them feel the enormity and the heinousness of their injustice and their cruelty, it would be necessary that one of those early usurers, who has been burning in Hell for the past three or four thousand years, should come back and give them a description of all the torments he is enduring and of the many injustices he committed which are the cause of what he suffers. No, these people are not part of my plan of instruction for you. They know very well that they are doing evil and that God will never pardon them unless they make restitution to those whom they have wronged. All that I could say to them would only serve to make them more guilty. So we will go carefully into something which involves an even greater number of people.

I tell you that wealth unjustly acquired will never enrich him who possesses it. On the contrary, it will become a source of trouble and evil for all his family. Oh, dear God, how blind man is! He is perfectly well aware that he is in the world for a brief space of time only. At every moment he sees people younger and stronger than himself passing out of it. It is all to no purpose: it does not help him to open his eyes. The Holy Ghost has told him plainly, through the mouth of the holy man Job, that he came into this world deprived of everything and that he will leave it the same way, that all the possessions he has cultivated will be taken from him at the moment when he least expects it: none of this serves to halt his progress. St. Paul affirms plainly that it will not be long before anyone who becomes rich through unjust means goes well astray onto the road of sin. And what is more, he will never see the face of God. That is so true that, without a miracle of grace, a miser, or if you prefer, a person who has acquired some wealth by fraud or cunning, will hardly ever be converted, so greatly does this sin blind anyone who commits it.

Listen to what St. Augustine says to those who have money which belongs to others. You can, he tells them, go to Confession, you can perform all the penance you like, you can weep for your sins, but unless you make restitution, whenever you can, God will never pardon you. . . . Either give back what is not yours, or you will have to make up your mind to go to Hell. The Holy Ghost does not stop at merely forbidding us to take and to covet the wealth of our neighbor—He does not wish us even to consider it or dwell upon it, lest we should want to lay our hands upon it. The prophet Zacharias tells us that the curse of the Lord will remain on the house of the thief until he is destroyed. And I am telling you that wealth acquired by fraud or by cunning will not only be of no profit but it will cause whatever you acquire legitimately to wither away and your days to be shortened.

My dear brethren, if I wanted to go into the conduct of all those who are present, I might perhaps find that I had only thieves. Does that amaze you? Just listen to me for a moment and you will realize that it is true. . . .

The most common thefts are those committed in the course of buying and selling. Let us examine this more closely so that you may recognize the wrong that you do and, at the same time, see how you can set about correcting it. When you bring along your produce to sell it, people ask you if your eggs and your butter are fresh. You hasten to answer in the affirmative, even though you know that the opposite is the truth. Why do you say that, unless it is to rob two or three pennies from some poor person who has had, perhaps, to borrow them to keep her house going? Another time it will be in the selling of a crop. You will take the precaution of putting the smallest and the poorest specimens in the midst of the bunch. You will possibly say: "But if I didn't do that, I wouldn't sell so much."

To put it another way, if you conducted yourself like a good Christian, you would not rob as you do. On another occasion, when counting your money, you will have noticed that you have been given too much, but you have said nothing: "So much the worse for the person concerned. It's not my fault."

Ah, my dear children, a day will come when you will possibly be told, and with more reason, "So much the worse for you!"

Someone wants to buy corn, or wine, or animals from you. He asks you if this corn is from a good year's crop. Without hesitation, you assure him that it is. You have mixed your wine with another of poorer quality, yet you sell it as a good and unadulterated wine. If people show signs of not believing you, you will swear that it is good, and it is not once but twenty times that you thus give your soul over to the Devil. Ah, my children, there is no need for you to be overanxious to give yourselves to him—you have been his for a long time now!

"What about this animal?" someone else will ask you. "Has it any defects? Don't cheat me now. I have only borrowed this money and if you do I will be in terrible difficulties."

"Oh, indeed no!" you will break in. "This is a very good animal. In fact, I am very sorry to be selling it. If I could do anything else I would not sell it at all."

In fact, of course, you are selling it because it is worth nothing at all and is no longer of any use to you.

"I do the same as everyone else. So much the worse for anyone who is taken in. I have beeen cheated; I try to cheat in my own turn; otherwise I would lose too much."

Is it, my children, that if others are damning themselves, then you must needs damn yourselves also? They are going to Hell —must you then go along with them? You would prefer to have a few extra pennies and go to Hell for all eternity? Very well. I am telling you, though, that if you have sold an animal with hidden faults, you are obliged to compensate the buyer for the loss which these defects have caused him; otherwise you will be damned.

"Ah, if you were in our place you would do the very same as we do."

Yes, my dear children, without any doubt I would do the very same as you do if, as you do, I wanted to be damned. But since I want to be saved, I would do the exact opposite of what you do.

১ঃ *IF YOU KNOW HOW TO GIVE, YOU MUST KNOW HOW TO PAY BACK*

THERE ARE PLENTY OF PEOPLE WHO, WHEN THEY are passing through a meadow or a turnip field or an orchard, will find no difficulty in filling their pockets with herbs or turnips and carrying away any amount of fruit in their baskets. Parents who see their children coming in with their hands full of these stolen objects simply laugh at them, saying, "Oh, my goodness, what grand things!"

My dear brethren, if you now take the value of a penny, and now the value of two pennies, you will soon have matter for a mortal sin. And after all, you can still commit mortal sin by taking less than your intention was to take....

Sometimes it will be a shoemaker who uses poor leather or

bad thread but who charges for his work as if it were of the best quality. Or again it may be a tailor who, under the pretext of not having received a sufficiently good price for his work, will keep a piece of his customer's material without saying anything about it. . . . Oh, dear Lord, how death will show up these thieves! . . .

Here is a weaver who spoils a part of his thread rather than go to the trouble of unraveling it. So he will use the smallest part of it and keep, without saying anything about it, what was entrusted to him. Then there is the woman, given some flax to spin, who will reject part of it on the pretext that it has not been well combed. Thus she will be able to keep some for herself, and then, by putting the thread into a damp place, she will be able to make right its weight. She gives no consideration to the fact that perhaps the thread belongs to a poor laborer to whom it will now be of no use because it is already half-ruined. She will thus be the cause of innumerable bad things which he will say against his master.

A shepherd knows quite well that he is not allowed to lead animals to pasture in a certain meadow or woods. That will not matter a bit to him; as long as he is not seen, this will do him very well. Another knows that he has been forbidden to go gathering tares in a certain cornfield because it is in bloom. He has a look around to see if anyone can see him, and then in he goes. Tell me, my brethren, would you be quite satisfied if your neighbor did that to you? No, certainly you would not! Very well, then, do you believe that this . . .[3]

Suppose we take a look at the conduct of laborers. Quite a large section of them are thieves. . . . If they are made to work for an agreed price, they will ruin half the job and they will continue until they get themselves paid. If they are hired by the day, they will be satisfied to work well while their employer is looking at them and after that they will give themselves over to talking and killing time. A servant will see no reason why he or

[3] Sentence incomplete.—Trans.

she should not receive and treat friends well during the absence of the owners of the house, knowing quite well that they would not allow this at all. Others will give away large alms in order to be considered charitable people. Should they not give these out of their own wages, which so often they squander on trifles? If this has happened to you, do not forget that you are obliged to pay back to the person concerned all that you gave to the poor without the knowledge or consent of your employers. Then again, there is the one who has been entrusted by his employer with the supervision of the staff, or of workmen, who gives out wine and all sorts of other things to them if they ask him. Understand this clearly: if you know how to give, you must know how to pay back. . . .

Suppose we turn now to the matter of masters—I know that we have no shortage of thieves in that quarter, either. How many masters do not, in actual fact, give as much money as they have agreed with their hired help to give? How many are there who, when they see the end of the year approaching, will do everything they possibly can to get their servants to leave so that they will not have to pay them. If an animal has died despite the care of the one in charge of it, they will keep back the price of it out of his wages, so that an unfortunate young fellow will have toiled the whole year through and at the end of his time will find himself with nothing at all. How many, again, have promised a suit length and will then have it made too narrow or of bad material or even will have the making of it put off for several years, to the point where they have to be brought to law to make them pay up? How many of them, when they are plowing or reaping or harvesting go beyond their own boundaries, or even cut a young sapling from their next-door neighbor's land to make themselves a handle for a scythe or a withe for a stook or to tie up a part of the cart? Had I not good reason to say, my dear brethren, that if we examine the conduct of most people we should find only thieves and cheats? . . .

There are very few of them, as you can see, who do not have something on their conscience. So, then, where are those who make restitution? I do not know any of them. . . .

Now, you will say, we can hope to know, roughly anyway, in what ways we can commit wrongs and injustices. But how, and to whom, must we make restitution?

You would like to make restitution? Very well, listen to me for a moment and you will know how to go about it. You must not be satisfied with paying back half, or three-quarters, but all, if you possibly can; otherwise you will be damned. There are some people who, without going into the question of the number of the people whom they have wronged, will give some alms or have some Masses said. And once that is done, they think they are quite safe. It is true, alms and Masses are all very well, but they must be given with your money and not with your neighbor's. That money was not yours; give it to its rightful owner and then give your own in alms and Masses if you want to: you will be doing very well. . . .

There are those who say: "I have wronged So-and-So, but he is quite rich enough; I know a poor person who has a much greater need of the money."

My good friend, give to this poor person from your own money, but pay back to your neighbor whatever substance you have taken from him.

"But he will put it to a bad use."

That has nothing to do with you. Give him his due, pray for him, and sleep well.

&❧ WINE IS HIS GOD

HABITUAL DRUNKENNESS IS NOT ONE OF THOSE SINS which time and grace will correct. To cure this sin, not an ordinary grace but a miracle of grace is required. You ask me why drunken people are so rarely converted. This is the reason: it is that they have neither faith, nor religion, nor pity, nor respect for holy things. Nothing is able to touch them or to open their eyes to their unhappy state. If you try to frighten them with death, or judgment, or the Hell which is waiting to consume them, if you talk to them of the happiness which God is keeping for those who love Him, the only answer you will get is a sly little smile which means: "You think now that you are going to make me afraid, like you do the children, but I am not one of those people who fall for that."

But look at what this means. Such a person believes that when we are dead, everything is finished. His god is his wine and he abides by it. The wine which he drinks to excess, the Holy Ghost warns him, is like a snake whose bite is death.

You believe none of this now, but in Hell you will learn that there was a God other than your stomach. . . .

It is essential for the habitual drunkard to get out of this state in order that he may understand the full horror of it. But, unfortunately, he has no faith. He believes only very weakly in the truths which the Church teaches us. It is essential for him to have recourse to prayer, but he hardly says any prayers at all, or if he does, it will be while he is dressing or undressing, or again, he may be satisfied to make just the Sign of the Cross, after a fashion, as he throws himself down on his bed, like a horse in its stable. It is essential that he should frequent the Sacraments, which are, in spite of the contempt with which the impious regard them, the sole remedies which the mercy of God offers us to draw us to Him. But, unfortunately, he does not even know the dispositions which he ought to cultivate in order to receive them worthily or even the bare essentials which he should know in order to save his soul. If you want to question him about his state, he understands nothing about it, as his contradictory answers show. If at the time of a Jubilee, or of a

Mission, or something like that, he wants to keep up appearances, he will be content to tell barely the half of his sins, and, still burdened with the others, he will approach the altar. That is to say, he will commit sacrilege; that will satisfy him. Dear God, what a dreadful state is that of the habitual drunkard and how hard it is to be able to leave it!

The Prophet Isaias tells us that habitual drunkards are useless as far as the doing of good on earth is concerned but that they are very dangerous when it comes to the doing of evil. To convince ourselves of that, my dear brethren, go into a cabaret, which St. John Climacus calls the Devil's Shop, the school where Hell holds forth and teaches its doctrine, the place where souls are sold, where homes are ruined, where health deteriorates, where quarrels begin, and where murders are committed. . . . What do you learn there? You know that better than I do. . . .

Take a look at this poor drunkard, my dear brethren. He is full of wine and his purse is empty. He throws himself down on a bench or a table. He is amazed in the morning to find himself still in the cabaret, when he thought that he was at home. He takes himself off after having spent all his money, and often, in order to be able to leave, he is forced to leave his hat or coat in pledge for the wine he has drunk. When he arrives home, his poor wife and their children, whom he has left without bread, and only their eyes to weep with, have to take flight from him unless they want to be ill treated, as if they were the cause of his spending all his money and getting his affairs into the bad state in which they are. Ah, dear Lord, how deplorable is the state of the habitual drunkard!

The Council of Mayence [Mainz] wisely tells us that a drunkard breaks the Ten Commandments of God. . . .

It is greatly to be feared that those who are gripped by this vice never cure themselves of it! . . .

Let us pray to the all-merciful God to preserve us from it. . . .

❧ ALL THAT YOU SAY "OVER AND ABOVE THESE IS OF EVIL"

IT IS INDEED SURPRISING, MY DEAR BRETHREN, THAT God should have had to give us a commandment forbidding us to profane His sacred name. Can you imagine, my children, that Christians could so hand themselves over to the Devil as to allow him to make use of them for execrating God, Who is so good and so benevolent? Can you imagine that a tongue which has been consecrated to God by holy Baptism, and so many times moistened by His adorable Blood, could be employed in vilifying its Creator? Would anyone be able to do that who truly believed that God had given him his tongue so that he might bless Him and sing His praises? You will agree with me that this is an abominable crime, one which would seem to urge God to overwhelm us with all sorts of evils and to abandon us to the Devil, whom we have been obeying with so much zeal. It is a sin which makes the hair stand on end in anyone who is not entirely lost to the Faith.

And yet, in spite of its enormity, its horror, its blackness, is there a more common sin than swearing, than the uttering of blasphemies, imprecations, and curses? Do we not all have the sorrow of hearing such language coming from the mouths of children who hardly know their *Our Father*, horrible words which are sufficient to draw down all sorts of evils upon a parish?

I am going to explain to you, my dear brethren, what is understood by swearing, blasphemy, profanities, imprecations, and curses. Try to sleep well during this period so that when the day of judgment comes, you will be found to have committed this evil without knowing what you were doing—though, of course, you will be damned because your ignorance will all be your own fault!

For you to understand the enormity of this sin, my brethren, it would be necessary for you to understand the enormity of the outrage which it does to God—a thing which no mortal can ever understand. No, my dear brethren, only the anger, the power and the wrath of God concentrated in the inferno of Hell can bring home to us the enormity of this sin. No, no, my children, let us not run this risk—there must be Hell for all eternity for this sin. All I want to do is to make you understand the difference which exists between swearing, blasphemy, profanity, imprecations, curses, and coarse words. A great many people confuse these things and take one thing for the other, which is the reason why they almost never accuse themselves of the sins they should, why they lay themselves open to the danger of bad confessions and therefore of damnation.

The Second Commandment, which forbids us to use false and unnecessary oaths or to perjure ourselves, is expressed in the following words: "Thou shalt not take the name of the Lord thy God in vain." This is as though God told us: I order you and command you to revere this name because it is holy and adorable. I forbid you to profane it by employing it to authorize falsehood, injustice, or even—without sufficient reason—the truth itself.

And Jesus Christ tells us not to swear in any way.

I tell you that badly instructed people often confuse blasphemy with swearing. If things have gone wrong with him, a man may, in a moment of anger, or rather of fury, say: "God is not just to make me suffer...."

Although by these words he has thus spoken profanely about God, he will confess his sin by saying: "Father, I accuse myself of swearing."

Yet it is not an oath but a blasphemy which he has uttered.

Someone is falsely accused of a fault which he has not committed. To support his protestations he will say: "May I never see the face of God if I did it!"

This is not an oath but a horrible imprecation. These are two sins which are every bit as bad as swearing. Another, who will have told his next-door neighbor that he is a thief, a scoundrel, will confess that he "has sworn at his neighbor." This is not swearing; it is using insulting language. Another will say foul and unseemly things and, in Confession, will accuse himself of "having spoken wrongly." He is wrong; he must say that he has been uttering obscenities.

My dear brethren, this is what swearing is: it is calling upon God to witness what we say or promise; and perjury is an oath which is false—that is to say, it is perjury to swear to what is not true.

The name of God is so holy, so great, and so adorable that the angels and the saints, St. John tells us, say unceasingly in Heaven: "Holy, holy, holy, is the great God of hosts; may His holy name be blessed for ever and ever." When the Blessed Virgin went to visit her cousin Elizabeth and the saintly woman said to her, "How happy you are to have been chosen to be the mother of God!" the Blessed Virgin replied to her: "He that is mighty hath done great things to me, and holy is His name."

We ought, you see, my dear brethren, to have a great respect for the name of God and pronounce it only with tremendous veneration and never in vain. St. Thomas tells us that it is a serious sin to pronounce the name of God in vain, that it is not a sin like other sins. In other sins the light nature of the matter diminishes the seriousness of and the malice in them, and quite often what could be a mortal sin is only a venial one. For instance, larceny is a mortal sin, but if it is larceny of something very small, like a couple of pennies, then it will be a venial sin only. Anger and gluttony are mortal sins, but slight anger or a little gluttony are only venial sins. In regard to swearing, however, it is not the same thing at all; here the lighter the matter, the greater the profanity. The reason for this is that the lighter the matter, the greater is the irreverence, as if a person were to ask the king to serve as a witness to some trifle, which would be to make a fool of him and to belittle him. Almighty God tells us.

that anyone who swears by His name will be sternly punished. We read in Holy Scripture that in the time of Moses there were two men, of whom one swore by the holy name of God. He was seized and brought before Moses, who asked God what should be done with him. The Lord told Moses to bring the man into a field and to command all those who had been witnesses of this blasphemy to put their hands upon his head and to stone him to death in order to do away with the blasphemer in the very midst of all his own people.

The Holy Scripture tells us again that whoever is accustomed to swearing, his house will be filled with iniquities and the curse will never leave the house until it has been destroyed. Our Lord Jesus Christ tells us in the Gospel not to swear by Heaven nor by earth because neither the one nor the other belongs to us. When you want to confirm something say: "That is," or "that is not." "Yes," or "no." "I did it," or "I did not do it."

Everything you say over and above that comes from the Devil. Besides, anyone who is in the habit of swearing is a fiery, undisciplined sort of person, very much wrapped up in his own feelings and always ready to swear as well as to a lie as to the truth.

But, you may say to me, if I do not swear, no one will believe me.

You are wrong. People never believe someone who swears because swearing presupposes someone who has no religion, and a person without religion is not worthy of being believed. There are many people who do not know how to sell the smallest article without swearing, as if their oath guaranteed the quality of their merchandise. If people see a merchant who swears oaths while he is selling, they immediately think that he is a person of bad faith and that they must be on their guard against being cheated. His oaths provoke only disgust and no one believes him. On the contrary, a person who does not swear adds good faith to what he is telling us.

We read in history of an example reported by Cardinal Bellarmine,[4] who showed us that oaths achieve nothing. There were, he tells us, two merchants in Cologne who seemed to be able to sell nothing without swearing. Their pastor strongly urged them to give up this bad habit, for, far from losing, they would gain much by doing so. They followed his counsel. However, for a while they did not sell very much. They went to find their pastor, telling him that they were not selling as much as he had given them to hope that they would. Their pastor said to them: "Have patience, my children, you may be quite sure that God will bless you."

In fact, at the end of a certain time, they were doing so very well that one might have thought, from the crowds that came to them, that they were giving their goods away. They themselves then saw that God had indeed blessed them in a very special way. The same Cardinal tells us that there was a good mother of a family who was very much in the habit of swearing. By dint of being persuaded that these oaths were unseemly in a mother and could but draw down curses upon her household, she was induced to correct this habit. She declared that since giving up this bad habit she had seen for herself that everything had gone well for her and that God had blessed her in a special manner.

Would you, my dear brethren, desire to be happy during your lives and to have God bless your homes? Take care, then, never to swear, and you will see that all will go well with you. God tells us that on the house wherein swearing holds sway the curse of the Lord will fall and that it will be destroyed. So why, my dear brethren, do you allow yourselves to fall into this evil way of behaving when God forbids it under the pain of making us unhappy in this world and of damning us in the next? Alas, if we would but understand in some small way what it is that we are doing! We will understand it—but then it will be too late.

In the second place, I say that there is an even worse form of

[4] St. Robert Bellarmine. He was not canonized until 1931.—Trans.

swearing. This occurs when to the oath there are added such execrations as would make you tremble with fear. Thus there are those unfortunate people who will say: "If what I am saying is not true, may I never see the face of God!"

Ah, unfortunate wretch, you are taking but too great a risk of never seeing it!

"If it is not true, may I lose my place in Heaven! May God damn me! May the Devil carry me off! . . ."

Alas, for you, my friend, hardened in this habit! The Devil will only too surely carry you off without your giving yourself to him so far in advance. How many others are there who invariably have the Devil ready on their tongues at the least annoyance: "Oh, this child is a devil . . . this devil of a beast . . . this devilish work . . . I wish it were obliterated, it drives me so mad!"

It is to be greatly feared that the person who has the Devil so often on his lips has him in his heart also! Then how many others are forever saying such things as: "On my soul, yes. . . . On my faith, no. . . . By Heaven! . . ." Or again: "Oh, God, yes! . . . Oh, God, no! . . . So help me. . . ."

There is another kind of swearing and of cursing to which people give little thought—these are the oaths which are uttered by the heart. There are those who believe that because they are not actually said by the mouth, there is no harm in them. You are greatly mistaken in that, my friends. It may happen that someone does some damage to your land, or elsewhere, and you swear at him in your heart and curse him inwardly, saying: "May the Devil make away with him! . . . May the elements destroy him! . . . May his food poison him! . . ."

And you keep these thoughts in your heart for any length of time and you think that because you do not actually say them with your lips there is no harm in them. My good friends, this is a very serious sin, and you must confess it or you will be lost. Alas, how few people know the state of their poor souls and how they appear in the eyes of God!

In the third place, we say that there are others even more guilty of this sin who swear, not only in respect of things which are true, but even in respect of things which are false. If you could understand how greatly your impiety and blasphemy insults God, you would never have the courage to commit this sin. You behave towards God as would the humblest slave who should say to the king: "Sire, you must serve me as a false witness."

Does not that fill you with horror, my dear brethren? God says to us in Holy Scripture: Be holy because I am holy. Do not lie and do not cheat or wrong your neighbor, and do not perjure yourselves by taking the name of the Lord your God for a witness to a lie, and do not profane the name of the Lord. St. John Chrysostom tells us: If it is already a great crime to swear to something true, what is the enormity of the crime of the man who swears falsely to confirm a lie? The Holy Ghost tells us that he who utters lies will perish. The Prophet Zacharias assures us that the curse will come to the house of the person who swears to confirm a lie and that it will remain thereon until that house is overthrown and destroyed. St. Augustine tells us that perjury is a fearful crime and a ferocious beast which creates appalling havoc. And what about the people who even add to this sin? For there are those who will couple with their perjury an oath of execration by saying such things as: "If that is not true, may I never see the face of God! . . . May God damn me! . . . May the Devil make away with me! . . .

Unhappy creatures! If the good God were to take you at your word, where would you be? For how many years already would you have been burning in the flames of Hell? Tell me, my children, can you really imagine that a Christian could deliberately be guilty of such a crime, of such horror? No, my dear brethren, no, it is inconceivable conduct on the part of a Christian.

You must examine your consciences as to whether you have had the determination to swear or to take a false oath and how many times you have had this thought—that is to say, how many times you have been disposed to do it. A great number of Christians do not give even a thought to this, although it is a serious sin.

Yes, you will say to me, I thought of it, but then I did not do it.

But your heart did it, and since you were in the disposition to do it, you were guilty in the eyes of God. Alas, poor religion, how little is known of you!

We encounter in history a striking example of the punishment of those who swear false oaths. In the time of St. Narcissus, Bishop of Jerusalem, three young libertines, who were abandoned to impurity, horribly calumniated their holy bishop, accusing him of crimes of which they themselves were guilty. They went before the judges and said that their bishop had committed such and such a sin, and they confirmed their testimony with the most appalling oaths. ·

The first said: "If I am not speaking the truth, let me be smothered."

The second: "If that is not true, I would be burned alive."

The third: "If that is not true, let me lose my eyes."

The justice of God was not slow in punishing them. The first was smothered and died horribly. In the case of the second, his house was set on fire by a burning brand from a bonfire in the town, and he was burned alive. The third, although he was punished, was happier than the others: he recognized his sin, did penance for it, and wept so much that he lost his sight.

Here is another example which is no less striking. We read in the history of the reign of St. Edward, King of England, that the Count Gondevin,[5] who was the king's father-in-law, was so jealous and so proud that he could not get along with anyone in the king's court. One day the King accused him of having had a hand in his brother's death.

[5] Earl Godwin (990-1053), father of Harold II, last of the Saxon kings of England.—Trans.

"If that is so," replied the Count, "may this piece of bread choke me."

With an open mind, the King took the piece of bread and made the Sign of the Cross over it. The other tried to eat the bread, but it stuck in his throat and choked him, and he died on the spot. You will agree with me, my dear brethren, after hearing these terrifying examples, that this sin must be very dreadful in the eyes of God for Him to want to punish it in so terrible a way.

Yet there are fathers and mothers, masters and mistresses, who at every moment of the day have these words on their lips: "Oh, what a dirty little swine! . . . Ah, you little beast! . . . Oh, you fool! . . . I wish you'd die here and now, you annoy me so much! . . . You couldn't be far enough away from me for my liking! . . . You'll have a lot to answer for! . . ."

(And, while I think of it, being foul-mouthed has a very close connection with cursing, too.)

Yes, my dear brethren, there are parents who have so little religion that such words are always on their lips. Alas, how many poor children are weak and feeble of soul, sour—vicious even—as a result of the curses that their fathers and mothers laid upon them!

We read in history that there was a mother who said to her child: "I wish you were dead, you are annoying me so much."

This unfortunate child fell dead at her feet.

Another mother said to her son: "May the Devil take you!"

The child disappeared without anyone knowing where he had gone or what had become of him. Dear God, what tragedy! Tragedy for the child and for the mother!

There once lived a man well respected for his steady living who, returning one day from a journey, called his servant in a very offhand manner, saying to him: "Here, you, you old devil of a valet! Come and get my boots off!" Immediately his boots began to draw themselves off without anyone touching them.

He was absolutely terrified and started to cry out: "Go away, Satan! It wasn't you I called, but my valet!"

So much did he cry out that the Devil fled there and then and his boots stayed half pulled off. This instance shows us, my dear brethren, how closely the Devil hovers around us, waiting to cheat us and cause us to lose our souls whenever the opportunity presents itself. It was for this reason that, as we see, the first Christians had such a horror of the Devil that they did not even dare to pronounce his name. You should take great care, then, never to say it yourself and never to allow your children or your servants to say it either. If you do hear them saying it, you must reprove them until you see that they have given up the habit altogether.

Now, my dear children, it is not only an evil thing to swear oneself, but it is also very wrong to make others swear. St. Augustine tells us that anyone who is the cause of another's swearing falsely in law is more guilty than someone who commits homicide because, he says, whoever kills a man kills his body only, whereas anyone who makes another swear falsely in law kills his soul. To give you an idea of the seriousness of this sin, I am going to show how guilty anyone is who foresees that people he intends to bring to law are going to perjure themselves. We read in history that there was a citizen of the town of Hippo, a man of some standing, but a little too attached to the things of this world. He decided to force a man who was in his debt to go to law. This wretch swore falsely, or in other words, he declared on oath that he owed nothing. The following night the man who had forced the law suit in order that he might be paid was himself brought before a tribunal where he saw a judge who spoke to him in a terrible and threatening voice and demanded to know why he had caused a man to perjure himself, why he should not have preferred to lose whatever was owed to him than to damn a soul. He was told, however, that since he had been given grace on this occasion, because of his works, he would be condemned to be beaten with rods. The following day his body was indeed covered with blood.

But, you may say to me, if we do not force people to swear in law, we shall lose our debts.

But would you rather lose someone's soul—and your own—than lose your money? Besides, my dear brethren, you may be very sure that if you make a sacrifice, in order not to offend God, He will not fail to recompense you in some other way.

Meanwhile, this does not very often happen, but you must be on your guard against giving presents to or canvassing people, who are to testify against you in law, not to speak the truth; that way you would damn them and yourselves. If you have done that and someone has had a wrong judgment given against him because of your falsehood, you would be obliged to repair all the harm that has been done and to compensate the person concerned, whether in his pocket or in his reputation, and to the fullest extent that you possibly can; otherwise you will be damned. You must also contemplate whether you have even considered swearing falsely and how many times you have entertained such a thought. There are some who believe that because they have said nothing, they have not, therefore, done any harm. My good friends, although you did not actually say anything, you committed a sin, since you were disposed to do the wrong. Consider, too, whether you have not ever given bad advice to others. Someone says to you: "I think I am going to be brought to court by So-and-So. What do you think about it? I have a great mind not to say what I saw, so that he may not lose the action; the other has more than enough to pay the costs. And yet at the same time I am doing something wrong."

You say to him: "Ah, yes, but the wrong is not very great. . . . You would make him lose too much. . . ."

If after that he perjures himself, and he himself has not enough to compensate the injured party, you are bound, because it was on your advice that the injury was done, to make the restitution yourself. Would you, my dear brethren, know what to do, both in law and in other affairs? Listen to Jesus Christ Himself when He tells us: "And if a man will contend with thee in the judgment, and take away thy coat, let go thy cloak also unto him," for that is more advantageous than going to law. Alas, that the machinery of justice should be the cause of the commission of sin! How many souls indeed are damned by such false oaths, by hatreds, by cheating, and by vengeance!

But think of those oaths, my dear brethren, which are most frequently uttered—which are uttered, indeed, at every hour of the day. If we tell something to someone and he does not believe us, we must needs swear to our statement with an oath. Fathers and mothers, masters and mistresses, should be on their guard against this. It often happens that children or servants have committed some fault and they are urged to admit it. Both children and servants may have a fear of being smacked or rebuked, so they will swear any number of times that what is alleged is not true, "may they never stir from that place if it is," and so on. It would be much more praiseworthy for those in authority to say nothing and to suffer any loss rather than make their subordinates damn themselves. Besides, where does that kind of thing get you? You all offend God, and you have nothing to show for it. What regret you would have, my dear brethren, if on the day of judgment you saw those souls damned because of some trifle or passing vanity of yours.

There are still others who swear or promise to do something or to give something to another without having the slightest intention of doing or giving it. Before they promise something, they had better consider whether they will be able to fulfill it. You should never say, before promising something, "If I don't do that now, may I never see God . . . may I never stir from this place."

Take care, my brethren! These sins are more horrible than you will ever understand. If, for example, during a fit of anger, you vowed to be revenged, it is quite clear that not only should you not do such a thing but that, on the contrary, you should ask pardon from God for having such a thought. The Holy Ghost tells us that anyone who swears will be punished. . . .

Now, you may ask me, what is to be understood by that word blasphemy? . . . This, my dear children, is so horrible a sin that it would not seem possible that Christians should ever have the courage to commit it. Blasphemy is a word which connotes the hating and cursing of infinite beauty, which explains why this sin directly attacks God. St. Augustine tells us: "We blaspheme when we attribute to God anything which is not an attribute of God or which is not in keeping with Him, or if we dare to take from what would be in keeping with Him, or, finally, if we attribute to ourselves that which is in keeping with God and which belongs to Him alone."

I tell you, therefore, that we blaspheme:

1. When we say that God is not just in making some people so rich that they have everything in abundance while so many others are so wretched that they have difficulty in getting bread to eat.

2. When we say that He is not as good as people say, since He allows so many people to remain weak and despised by others while there are some who are loved and respected by everyone.

3. Or if we say that God does not see everything, that He does not know what is going on in the world.

4. If we say: "If God shows mercy to So-and-So, He is not just because that man has done too much harm."

5. Or again, when we come up against some loss or setback and we lose our temper with God and say such things as: "Ah, but I certainly have bad luck! God cannot do any more to me! I believe that He does not even know I am in the world, or if He does know, it is only so that He can make me suffer!"

It is also blasphemy to criticize the Blessed Virgin and the Saints by saying such things as: "That one has not much power! I don't know how many prayers I have said to him (or her), and I have never got anything."

St. Thomas tells us that blasphemy is an insulting and outrageous utterance against God or the saints. This may be done in four ways:

1. By affirmation, as when we say: "God is cruel and unjust to allow me to suffer so many wrongs, to allow anyone to calumniate me like that, to allow me to lose that money or this lawsuit. I am very unfortunate! Everything is going wrong with me. I cannot have anything, while everything is going well with other people."

2. It is blasphemy to say that God is not all-powerful and that one can do anything without Him. It was blasphemy for Sennacherib, the King of the Assyrians, to besiege the town of Jerusalem, saying that in spite of God he would take the town. He mocked at God, saying that He was not powerful enough to stop him from entering the town and putting it to fire and the sword. But God, in order to punish this wretched man and to show him that He was indeed all-powerful, sent an angel who in one single night killed one hundred and eighty thousand of his men. On the following morning, when the King saw his army massacred and did not know by whom, he was terrified and fled to Nineveh, where he himself was killed by his own two children.

3. It is blasphemy to bestow upon some creature that which is due God alone, like those unhappy creatures who will say to some sinful creature, who is the object of their passions: "I love you with all the fervor of my heart. . . . I worship you. . . . I adore you." This is a sin which provokes horror, and yet is at least common enough in practice.

4. It is horrible blasphemy to damn something in the name of God.

This sin of blasphemy is so great and so hideous in the eyes of God that it draws down all sorts of evils upon the world. The Jews had such a horror of blasphemies that when they heard anyone blaspheming, they rent their garments. They did not dare even to pronounce the word but called it "Benediction."

The holy man Job had such fear that his children had blasphemed that he offered sacrifices to God in case they had. . . . St. Augustine says that those who blaspheme Jesus Christ in Heaven are more cruel than those who crucified Him on earth. The bad thief blasphemed Jesus Christ when He was on the Cross, saying: "If thou be Christ, save thyself and us." The Prophet Nathan said to King David: "Because thou hast given occasion to the enemies of the Lord to blaspheme, for this thing, the child that is born to thee shall surely die." God tells us that whoever blasphemes the name of the Lord shall die. We read in Holy Scripture that the people brought a man to Moses who had blasphemed. Moses consulted the Lord, who told him that he must have the man brought to a field and put to death, that is to say, stoned to death.

We can say that blasphemy is truly the language of Hell. St. Louis, King of France, had such a horror of this sin that he ordained that all blasphemers should be branded on the forehead. An important person from Paris, who had blasphemed, was brought to the King and several people interceded for him, but the King said that he would die himself in order to wipe out this dreadful sin, and he ordered that the man should be punished. The tongues of those who were wicked enough to commit this crime were cut out by order of the Emperor Justin. During the reign of Robert, the kingdom of France was overwhelmed by all kinds of evils, and God revealed to a Saint that while the blasphemies continued, the chastisements would continue, too. A law was enacted which condemned all those who blasphemed to have their tongues pierced with a red-hot iron for the first offense and ordered that on the second offense they should be executed.

Be warned, my dear brethren, that if blasphemy reigns in your homes, all therein will perish. St. Augustine tells us that blasphemy is an even greater sin than perjury because, as he says, by perjury we take the name of God in witness of something which is false, whereas in blasphemy we are saying something false of God. What a crime is this! And who amongst us has ever fully understood it? St. Thomas, again, tells us that there is another kind of blasphemy against the Holy Ghost which can be committed in three ways:

1. By attributing to the Devil the works of Almighty God, as did the Jews when they said that Jesus Christ drove out devils in the name of the prince of devils, as did the tyrants and persecutors who attributed to the Devil and to magic the miracles performed by the saints.

2. It is blasphemy against the Holy Ghost, St. Augustine tells us, to die in final impenitence. Impenitence is a spirit of blasphemy, since the remission of our sins is achieved through love, which is the Holy Ghost.

3. We blaspheme when we perform actions which are directly opposed to the goodness of God—as when we despair of our salvation and yet are not willing to take the necessary steps to obtain it; as when we are angered because others receive more graces than we do. Take great care never to allow yourselves to fall into these kinds of sins because they are so very horrible! In this way we look upon Almighty God as unjust because He gives more to others than He does to us.

Have you never blasphemed, my dear brethren, by saying that Providence is only for the rich and the wicked? If something went wrong with your affairs, have you not blasphemed by saying: "But what did I do to God more than anyone else that I should have so much to put up with?"

What have you done, my friend? Lift up your eyes and you will see Him whom you have crucified. Have you not blasphemed, also, by saying that you were tempted beyond measure, that you could not do otherwise, that this was your lot? . . . Well, my dear brethren, did you never think along these lines? . . . So it is God who would have had you vicious, bad tempered, violent . . . fornicators, adulterers, blasphemers! You do not believe in Original Sin, which dragged men down from the state of uprightness and justice in which we were all at first created!

It is stronger than you are. . . . But, my friends, did religion never come, then, to your aid to help you to understand all the corruption of Original Sin? And yet you dare, wretched sinner, to blaspheme against Him Who gave religion to you as the greatest gift which He could make you!

Have you not also blasphemed against the Blessed Virgin and the saints? Have you not laughed at their virtues, at their penances and their miracles? Alas! In this evil century how many impious people do we not find who carry their impiousness to the point of actually scoffing at the Saints, who are in Heaven, and the just, who are on earth? How many are there who make fun of the austerities which the Saints practiced and who neither wish to serve God themselves nor tolerate that anyone else should serve Him either? Look again, my dear brethren, and see if you have uttered your swearing and your blasphemy to children. Unhappy people, what chastisements await you in the next life!

What is the difference, you may ask me, between blasphemy and the repudiation of God? There is a very big difference, my dear brethren, between blasphemies and repudiations of God. Now in speaking about repudiation, I do not want to talk about those people who repudiate God by abandoning the true religion. We call such people renegades or apostates. But I do want to talk about those people who, when they are speaking, have the dreadful habit, whether in sudden vexation or real passion, of attacking the holy name of God. For example, someone who has lost on a sale or on a gamble will inveigh against God as if he wanted to convince himself that God was the cause of his misfortune. If something happens to you, it seems that God should bear the brunt of all the fury of your resentment, as if God were the cause of your loss or of the accident which befell you. Unhappy sinner! He Who created you from nothing, Who preserves you, and Who fills you continually with blessings and gifts—it is He whom you dare just the same to mock, to profane His holy name and to repudiate, while He, if He had been swayed solely by His justice, would long ago have consigned you to the flames of Hell.

We see that anyone who has the misfortune to commit these very grave sins usually comes to a bad end. There is an account of a man who was very ill and reduced to dire want. A missionary went to his home to see him and to hear his Confession, and to him the sick man said: "Father, God is punishing my outbursts of anger and rages, my blasphemies, and my repudiations of Him. I have been ill for quite a long time. I am very poor; all my wealth has come to a bad end. My children despise and abandon me; they are worthless because of the bad example I have given them. Already now for quite some time I have been suffering, lying here on this wretched bed. My tongue is all diseased and I cannot swallow anything without experiencing terrible agony. Alas, Father, I am very much afraid that after all this suffering in this world, I will still have to suffer in the next."

We see even in our own day that all those people who swear and profane the holy name of God almost always come to bad ends. Take good heed, my dear brethren, if you have this evil habit. You had better correct it, for fear that if you do not do penance for it in this world, you will be doing it in Hell. Never lose sight of the fact that your tongue should be employed in praying to God and in singing His praises. If you have the evil habit of swearing, you should often, in order to purify your lips, say the holy name of Jesus with great respect.

Now perhaps you will ask me what is understood by cursing and the uttering of imprecations. It means, my dear brethren, cursing a person or a thing or an animal in moments of anger or despair. It is wishing to destroy him or to make him suffer. The Holy Ghost tells us that the person who has the ready curse in his mouth should greatly fear, lest God should grant him what he desires. There are some who have the Devil always on their tongues, who consign to him everything which annoys them. When they are at work, if an animal does not go the way they want it to, they will curse it and consign it to the Devil. There are others who, when the weather or the children do not behave as they would wish, call down maledictions upon one or the other. . . . Do not ever forget that the Holy Ghost tells us that a curse uttered irresponsibly or carelessly will fall upon someone. St. Thomas tells us that if we utter a curse against someone, the sin is mortal if we desire whatever it is we say to happen to that person. St. Augustine tells us that a mother cursed her children—there were seven of them. They were all possessed by the Devil. Many children, who have been cursed by their parents, have been delicate and wretched throughout their lives. We read that there was once a mother whose daughter had put her into such a temper that she cried out: "I wish your arm would wither on you!" In fact, this child's arm did wither, almost immediately.[6]

Married people should take great care never to utter these dreadful sayings to each other. There are some who, if they are unhappy in their homes, will curse their wives, their children, their parents, and all who in any way have any part in the marriage. Alas, my friends, the whole source of your unhappiness lies in yourself because you entered into marriage with a conscience quite steeped in sin. Think about that before Almighty God, and you will see that it is, in fact, the truth. Workers should never curse their work or those who make them work.

Besides, in any event, your imprecations will not make your affairs go any the better. On the contrary, if you have some patience, if you know how to offer up all your difficulties to God, you will bring yourself much nearer to Heaven.

Have you not also cursed the tools which serve you in your work, invoking maledictions upon them, your animals, and so on? That is the sort of thing, my dear brethren, which draws

---

[6] There is a note here by the Curé about hidden oaths, that is, using the name of God or the holy name of Jesus in contracted form or with the spelling slightly altered.—Trans.

down all sorts of evils upon your animals, upon your labors, and upon your lands, which are often ravaged by hailstorms, by drenching rains, and by frosts. Have you not indeed cursed yourselves: "Ah! I wish I had never seen the light of day. . . . I wish I had been born dead. . . . I wish I were back in oblivion." Alas! These are terrible sins, and quite a large number of people never accuse themselves of them in Confession or ever think about them. I will tell you yet again that you must never curse your children, your animals, your work, or the weather because in cursing all these things, you are cursing what Almighty God does by His holy will. Children should take care never to give occasion to their parents to curse them, which is the greatest of all evils. Often a child who is cursed by his parents is cursed by Almighty God. When someone has done something to you which has angered you very much, now instead of wishing him to the Devil, you would do far more good by saying to him: "May God bless you!" Then you would be a genuinely good servant of God who returns good for evil.   In connection with this Commandment, there yet remains to be said something in the matter of the vows which people make. You should be very careful never to make vows without taking proper counsel beforehand. There are some people who, when they are ill, dedicate themselves to all the saints and then later on do not go to the trouble to fulfill their promises. You should also be careful that you make these vows properly, that is to say, while you are in a state of grace. What a number of sins are committed in the matter of these vows! And the whole business, instead of pleasing God, can only offend Him!

If you were to ask me why it is that there are nowadays so many who swear, who take false oaths, who utter frightful curses and imprecations and repudiate God, I would reply that these same people, who give themselves up to such horrible practices, are those who have neither faith, nor religion, nor conscience, nor virtue. These are the people who, to a certain extent, are abandoned by God. How much happier we should be if we had the good fortune to employ our tongues, which have been consecrated to God by holy Baptism, solely in prayer to God, Who is so good, so benevolent, and to sing His praises! Since it is for that purpose that God has given us a tongue, let us try, my dear brethren, to consecrate it to Him, so that after this life we shall have the happiness of going to Heaven to bless Him for all eternity. This is what I desire for you.

֍ *THE DUTIES OF THE PREGNANT WOMAN*

I AM GOING TO TALK TO YOU AS SIMPLY AS I POSSIBLY can, so that you can easily understand what your duties are and carry them out. I tell you:

1. That as soon as a woman is pregnant, she should say some prayers or give some alms. Better still, if she can do so, she should have a Mass said to ask the Blessed Virgin to take her under her protection, so that she may obtain from God the blessing that this little child may not die without having received holy Baptism. If a mother truly had the religious spirit, she would say to herself: "Ah! If I could only be sure of seeing this little child becoming a saint, of seeing him for all eternity by my side, singing the praises of God! What a joy that would be for me!"

But no, my dear brethren, that is not the thought which occupies the mind of an expectant mother. She will experience, rather, a devouring resentment on beholding herself in this state and perhaps the thought of even destroying the fruit of her womb will come to her. Oh, dear God! Can the heart of a Christian mother conceive such a crime? Yet we shall see some of them who unashamedly will have entertained such homicidal thoughts!

2. I tell you that an expectant mother who wishes to preserve

her child for Heaven should avoid two things. The first is carrying loads which are too heavy and lifting her arms to take something; this could be injurious to her poor child and cause its death. The second thing to be avoided is the taking of remedies which could be too harsh on her child or which could heat her blood to an extent which could be fatal to it. Husbands should overlook a great many things which they would not put up with at any other time. If they will not do this for the sake of the mother, let them do it for the sake of the little child. For perhaps the child might lose the grace of Holy Baptism, which would be the greatest evil of all!

3. As soon as a mother sees her confinement approaching, she should go to Confession—and for many reasons. The first is that many women die during their confinements, and if she should have the misfortune to be in a state of sin, she would be damned. The second is that being in a state of grace, all the sufferings and the pains which she will endure will gain merit for Heaven. The third is that God will not fail to give her all the blessings which she will desire for her child. A mother at her confinement should preserve modesty as far as is possible in her state and never lose sight of the fact that she is in the presence of God and in the company of her Guardian Angel. She should never eat meat on the forbidden days without permission, a practice which would draw down punishment upon herself and her child.

4. A child should never be left longer than twenty-four hours without being baptized.

&ᴥ THE DUTIES OF THE MOTHER

YOU SHOULD NEVER HAVE YOUR CHILDREN SLEEPING with you from the time they are two years old. If you do, you are committing a sin. The Church did not make this law without reason. You are bound to observe it.

But, you will say to me, sometimes it is very cold or we are very tired.

All that, my dear brethren, is not a reason which could excuse you in the eyes of God. Besides, when you married, you knew quite well that you would be obliged to fulfill certain responsibilities and obligations which are attached to the married state. Still, my dear brethren, there are fathers and mothers who are so little instructed in their religion or who are so indifferent to their duties that they will have sleeping with them children from fifteen to eighteen years of age, and often brothers and sisters together. Dear Lord! These poor fathers and mothers are in a terrible state of ignorance!

But, you will say, we have no bed.

You have no bed? But it would be better to let them sleep on a chair or in a neighbor's house. Dear Lord! The parents and children who damn themselves!

But I will return to my subject and repeat to you that all the time that you allow your children to sleep with you after they have reached two years of age, you are offending God. How many mothers are there who have found their children smothered in the morning! How many mothers are present to whom this calamity has happened! And even if the good God has preserved you from it, you are no less guilty than if, every time your children slept with you, you found them smothered in the morning. You do not wish to agree with this, that is to say, you do not wish to correct it. We will wait until the Judgment, and you will be obliged to recognize what you do not wish to recognize today.

There are mothers who have so little religion or, if you like, are so ignorant that if they want to show off their baby to some neighboring mothers, they will show it to them naked. Others, when they are putting on diapers, will leave the babies, for a long period of time, uncovered before everyone. Now even if there is no one present at all, you should not do this. Should you not respect the presence of their Guardian Angels? It is the same thing when you are feeding them. Should any Christian mother allow her breasts to remain exposed? And even if they are covered, should she not turn aside to some place where there is no one else? Then there are others who, under the pretext of being foster-nurses, are continually only half-covered. This is very disgusting. It is enough to make even the pagans blush. People are compelled to avoid their company in order not to expose themselves to evil thoughts.

But, you will say to me, even if everyone is around, we must feed our children and change their diapers when they cry!

And I shall tell you that when they cry, you ought to do everything you possibly can to quieten them but that it is a far better thing to let them cry a little than to offend God. Alas! How many mothers are the cause of evil glances, of bad thoughts, of immodest touches! Tell me, are these the Christian mothers who should be so reserved? Oh, dear God! What judgment should they expect? Others are so cruel that they let their children run around for the whole morning, during the summer, only half-dressed. Tell me, unhappy people, would it not be better for you to take your places among the savage beasts? Where is your religion, then, and your anxiety to do your duty? Alas! As far as religion is concerned, you have none. As for your duties, have you ever known what they were? That you have not, you give proof every day. Ah, poor children, how unfortunate you are to belong to such parents!

&ᴥ *THE DUTIES OF PARENTS*

I WARNED YOU THAT YOU SHOULD BE SURE TO KEEP a watchful eye over your children when you send them out to the fields, for out there, far away from you, they can give themselves over to whatever the Devil may put into their minds. What if I dared to tell you that they carry on with all sorts of ugly and immodest practices, that they pass most of the day in all sorts of abominable ways? I know very well that the majority of them do not know the evil which they do—but wait until they do acquire that knowledge. At that moment the Devil will not fail to remind them of what they have done in order to make them commit that sin or others. Do you know, my dear brethren, what your negligence or your ignorance produces? Look at it, then, and keep it in mind. A large number of the children that you send out to the fields make their First Holy Communion sacrilegiously. They have contracted shameful habits, and either they dare not confess them or they do not give them up. Later, if a priest who does not wish to damn them refuses them absolution, people will reproach him and say: "That's because it's my child. . . ."

Go away, you wretched sinners, and watch a little more carefully over your children and they will not be refused. Yes, indeed, I am telling you that the great majority of your children began their bad ways and earned their later rejection during the time when they went out to the fields.

❧ YOU WILL ANSWER FOR THEIR SOULS

BUT, YOU WILL TELL ME, WE CANNOT BE ALWAYS following them around. We have other things to do.

As to that, my dear brethren, I will say nothing. All I know is that you will answer for their souls as much as for your own.

But we do all we can.

I do not know whether you do all you can, but this much I do know: if your children incur damnation at home with you, you, too, will be damned. That much I know, and nothing else. You may go on saying "No" to that, saying that I go too far. You will agree with it if you have not entirely lost your faith. That alone should suffice to cast you into a state of despair from which you could not emerge. But I know well that you will not take another step to fulfill any better your duties to your children. You are not at all disturbed, and you are almost right, for you will have plenty of time to torment yourselves during all eternity. We will pass on.

ᘏ❧ TO THEIR SHAME IT MUST BE SAID

YOU SHOULD NEVER PUT YOUR MAIDSERVANTS OR your daughters to sleep in quarters to which the men will be going in the morning looking for food. This is something which, to the shame of fathers and mothers, must be said. These unfortunate children, or servants, are confused and embarrassed getting up and dressing in front of people who have no more religion than if they had never heard anyone speak of the one true God. Often, even, the beds for these unfortunate people have no curtains around them.

But, you will say to me, if we had to do all the things you say, there would be an awful lot of work to do.

My friend, it is work which you must do, and if you do not do it, you will be punished on account of it: see. . . .

I know very well that you will do nothing, or practically nothing, in respect of what I have just been teaching you. But no matter. I will always continue to tell you what you ought to do. Then all the wrongdoing will be yours and not mine. . . . When God comes to judge you, you will not be able to say that you did not know what you should have done. . . .

I shall remind you of what I am telling you today.

ᘏ❧ GETTING TO KNOW THE RIGHT PEOPLE

YOU TALK TO THEM OF THE WORLD. A MOTHER WILL begin to tell her daughter that such and such a girl has married such and such a man, that she has done very well for herself, that the daughter ought now to see to it that she has the same good fortune. This type of mother has nothing in her head except her daughter—that is to say, she will do everything in her power to show her off to the eyes of the neighbors. She will deck her out in vanities, even perhaps to the extent of running herself into debt. She will teach her daughter to show herself to the best advantage while walking, telling her that she walks with such a slouch that no one would know what she is like. Are you surprised that there are mothers who are so blind? Alas! The number of these poor blind mothers who seek the loss of their daughters is very high.

You will see them then in the morning when their daughters are going out, and they are more concerned with seeing that their daughters' headgear is on straight, that their faces and hands are attractive and clean, than with asking them if they turned their hearts to God, if they have said their prayers and made their morning offering. Of all that, they say nothing at all. Then they will tell their daughters that they should not appear shy or awkward, that they should be charming to everyone, that they ought to be thinking about getting to know the right people in order to get themselves settled in life. How many mothers will you hear saying to their daughters: "If you are nice and pleasant now, or if you make a success of this or that, I will let you go to the fair at Montmerle or to the *vogue.*"[7] In other words, if you make a success of this or that, as I wish, I will drag you into Hell.

Oh, dear Lord! Is this really the language of Christian parents, who should pray day and night for their little children?

There is something which is even sadder than this, and that is the case of those daughters who are not at all interested in going out and about. The parents keep at them, entreating and encouraging them, saying: "You are always staying in. You will

[7] Local open-air festivals which had their culmination in an all-night dance and revel.—Trans.

never get yourself settled in life. You will let no one tell you anything about the world."

You would like your daughter to get to know people, my dear mother? Do not worry too much—she will get to know plenty of them without your having to upset yourself! Just wait a little while and you will see how well she will get to know them. . . .

You pushed her into it first of all, but it will not be you who will draw her back. You will weep, maybe, but what good will your tears do? None at all. . . .

ও YOU NO LONGER CONTROL THEM

EVERY DAY YOU ARE COMPLAINING ABOUT YOUR children, are you not? Your complaint is that you can no longer control them? That is very true. You have perhaps forgotten the day that you said to your son or your daughter: "If you want to go to the fair at Montmerle, or even to the *vogue* at the cabaret, you can go there. But you must come back early."

Your daughter told you that it would be just as you wished.

"Go along so; you never go out. You should have some moments of pleasure."

You will not say: "No!" Later on, you will have no need, either, to urge or even to give her permission to go. Then you will be in a terrible state because she has gone without telling you. Look back, my dear mother, and you will recall that you gave her the permission once . . . which was for all time. . . . You wanted her to get to know the right people so that she could get married and settle down. In fact, as the result of gadding about, she will get to know many people. . . .

Is not this the way, my dear mother? "Let the Pastor talk

away, go along just the same, be good, come back at an early hour, and all will be well." This is very good, my dear mother, but listen:

One day I found myself walking along near where a big fire was burning. I took a handful of very dry straw and I threw it into the fire, telling it not to burn. Those who watched what I was doing told me, as they laughed at me, "You do well to tell it not to burn. Nothing will stop it from burning."

"But how will that be," I answered, "when I told it not to?"

What do you think of that, my dear mother? Do you recognize yourself? Is not that exactly what you are doing? . . .

Tell me, my dear mother, if you have any sentiments of religion and of affection for your children, should you not be doing everything you possibly can to help them to avoid the evil that you did yourself when you were the same age as your own daughter? Let us put it a bit more bluntly. You are not sufficiently content with being unhappy yourself, but do you want your children to be unhappy, too?

And you, my daughter, you are unhappy in your own home? I am very distressed about that, I am very troubled by it, but I am less surprised than if you said you were happy, with all the pressure that is brought to bear upon you to get married.

Yes, my dear brethren, corruption among the young people today has grown to such a high degree that it would be almost as impossible to find among them those who worthily receive this Sacrament as it would be impossible to see a damned soul ascending to Heaven.

But, you will tell me, there are still some among them.

Alas, my friends, where are they? . . .

Ah, yes, fathers and mothers see no harm in leaving a girl with a young man for three or four hours in the evening, or even when they are out at Vespers.

But, you will say, they are very good.

Yes, without any doubt, they are very good. Charity urges us to believe that. But tell me this, my dear mother, were you so very good when you were in the same circumstances as your own daughter? . . .

Alas, it would seem today that if a young man or a young girl wish to settle down, it must follow that they abandon God. . . . No, we will not go into details; we will come back to that some other time. . . .

What I have said to you today amounts to only a glance at the subject. Come back on Sunday, fathers and mothers, leave your children to mind the house, and I will go further—without being able to get you to know half the significance of what I am saying!

Alas, what about you, you poor children! . . . Being your spiritual father, I give you this advice: When you see your parents, who miss religious services, who work on Sundays, who eat meat on the forbidden days, who do not go to the Sacraments any more, who do not improve their minds on religious matters—do the very opposite before them, so that your good example may save them, and if you are wise and good enough to do this, you will have gained everything. That is what I most desire for you.

੩૭ *HE WILL HELP US*

YES, MY DEAR BRETHREN, IN EVERYTHING THAT WE see, in everything that we hear, in all we say and do, we are conscious of the fact that we are drawn towards evil. If we are at table, there is sensuality, and gluttony, and intemperance. If we take a few moments of recreation, there are the dangers of flightiness and idle chatter. If we are at work, most of the time it is self-interest, or avarice, or envy which influences us—or even vanity. When we pray, there is negligence, distraction, distaste, and boredom. If we are in pain or any trouble, there are complaints and murmurings. When we are doing well and are prosperous, pride, self-love, and contempt for our neighbor take hold of us. Our hearts swell with pride when we are praised. Wrongs inflame us into rages.

There you see my dear brethren, the thing which made the greatest of the saints tremble. This was what made so many of them retire into the desert to live solitary lives; this was the source of so many tears, of so many prayers, of so many penances. It is true that the saints who were hidden away in the forests were not exempt from temptations, but they were far removed from so much bad example as that which surrounds us continually and which is the cause of so many souls being lost.

But, my dear brethren, we see from their lives that they watched, they prayed, and they were in dread unceasingly, while we, poor, blind sinners, are quite placid in the midst of so many dangers which could lose us our souls! Alas, my dear brethren, some of us do not even know what it is to be tempted because we hardly ever, or very rarely, resist. Which one of us can expect to escape from all these dangers? Which one of us will be saved? Anyone who wanted to reflect upon all these things could hardly go on living, so greatly terrified would he be! However, my dear brethren, what ought to console and reassure us is that we have to deal with a good Father Who will never allow our struggles to be greater than our strength, and every time we have recourse to Him, He will help us to fight and to conquer.

❧ WE MUST EXPECT TEMPTATION

IT IS MOST UNFORTUNATE FOR OURSELVES IF WE DO not know that we are tempted in almost all our actions, at one time by pride, by vanity, by the good opinion which we think people should have of us, at another by jealousy, by hatred and by revenge. At other times, the Devil comes to us with the foulest and most impure images. You see that even in our prayers he distracts us and turns our minds this way and that. It seems indeed that we are in a state . . . since we are in the holy presence of God.[8] And even more, since the time of Adam, you will not find a saint who has not been tempted—some in one way, some in another—and the greatest saints are those who have been tempted the most. If Our Lord was tempted, it was in order to show us that we must be also. It follows, therefore, that we must expect temptation. If you ask me what is the cause of our temptations, I shall tell you that it is the beauty and the great worth and importance of our souls which the Devil values and which he loves so much that he would consent to suffer two Hells, if necessary, if by so doing he could drag our souls into Hell.

We should never cease to keep a watch on ourselves, lest the Devil might deceive us at the moment when we are least expecting it. St. Francis tells us that one day God allowed him to see the way in which the Devil tempted his religious, especially in matters of purity. He allowed him to see a band of devils who did nothing but shoot their arrows against his religious. Some returned violently against the devils who had discharged them. They then fled, shrieking hideous yells of rage. Some of the arrows glanced off those they were intended for and dropped at their feet without doing any harm. Others pierced just as far as the tip of the arrow and finally penetrated, bit by bit.

If we wish to hunt these temptations away, we must, as St. Anthony tells us, make use of the same weapons. When we are tempted by pride, we must immediately humble and abase ourselves before God. If we are tempted against the holy virtue of purity, we must try to mortify our bodies and all our senses and to be ever more vigilant of ourselves. If our temptation consists in a distaste for prayers, we must say even more prayers, with greater attention, and the more the Devil prompts us to give them up, the more we must increase their number.

The temptations we must fear most are those of which we

[8] Sentence incomplete.—Trans.

are not conscious. St. Gregory tells us that there was a religious who for long had been a good member of his community. Then he developed a very strong desire to leave the monastery and to return to the world, saying that God did not wish him to be in that monastery. His saintly superior told him: "My friend, it is the Devil who is angry because you may be able to save your soul. Fight against him."

But no, the other continued to believe that it was as he claimed. St. Gregory gave him permission to leave. But when he was leaving the monastery, the latter went on his knees to ask God to let this poor religious know that it was the Devil who wanted to make him lose his soul. The religious had scarcely put his foot over the threshold of the door to leave when he saw an enormous dragon, which attacked him.

"Oh, brothers," he cried out, "come to my aid! Look at the dragon which will devour me!"

And indeed, the brethren who came running when they heard the noise found this poor monk stretched out on the ground, half-dead. They carried him back into the monastery, and he realized that truly it was the Devil who wanted to tempt him and who was bursting with rage because the superior had prayed for him and so had prevented the Devil from getting him. Alas, my dear brethren, how greatly we should fear, lest we do not recognize our temptations! And we shall never recognize them if we do not ask God to allow us to do so.

₰ *WE ARE NOTHING IN OURSELVES*

TEMPTATION IS NECESSARY TO US TO MAKE US RE-alize that we are nothing in ourselves. St. Augustine tells us that we should thank God as much for the sins from which He has preserved us as for those which He has had the charity to forgive us. If we have the misfortune to fall so often into the snares of the Devil, we set ourselves up again too much on the strength of our own resolutions and promises and too little upon the strength of God. This is very true.

When we do nothing to be ashamed of, when everything is going along according to our wishes, we dare to believe that nothing could make us fall. We forget our own nothingness and our utter weakness. We make the most delightful protestations that we are ready to die rather than to allow ourselves to be conquered. We see a splendid example of this in St. Peter, who told our Lord that although all others might be scandalized in Him, yet he would never deny Him.

Alas! To show him how man, left to himself, is nothing at all, God made use, not of kings or princes or weapons, but simply of the voice of a maidservant, who even appeared to speak to him in a very indifferent sort of way. A moment ago, he was ready to die for Him, and now Peter protests that he does not even know Him, that he does not know about whom they are speaking. To assure them even more vehemently that he does not know Him, he swears an oath about it. Dear Lord, what we are capable of when we are left to ourselves!

There are some who, in their own words, are envious of the saints who did great penances. They believe that they could do as well. When we read the lives of some of the martyrs, we would, we think, be ready to suffer all that they suffered for God; the moment is shortlived, we say, for an eternity of reward. But what does God do to teach us to know ourselves or, rather, to know that we are nothing? This is all He does: He allows the Devil to come a little closer to us. Look at this Christian who a moment ago was quite envious of the hermit who lived solely on roots and herbs and who made the stern resolution to treat his body as harshly. Alas! A slight headache, a prick of a pin, makes him, as big and strong as he is, sorry for himself. He is very upset. He cries with pain. A moment ago he would have been willing to do all the penances of the anchorites—and the merest trifle makes him despair!

Look at this other one, who seems to want to give his whole life for God, whose ardor all the torments there are cannot damp. A tiny bit of scandalmongering . . . a word of calumny . . . even a slightly cold reception or a small injustice done to him . . . a kindness returned by ingratitude . . . immediately gives birth in him to feelings of hatred, of revenge, of dislike, to the point, often, of his never wishing to see his neighbor again or at least of treating him coldly with an air which shows very plainly what is going on in his heart. And how many times is this his waking thought, just as it was the thought that almost prevented him from sleeping? Alas, my dear brethren, we are poor stuff, and we should count very little upon our good resolutions!

ह्ल BEWARE IF YOU HAVE NO TEMPTATIONS

WHOM DOES THE DEVIL PURSUE MOST? PERHAPS you are thinking that it must be those who are tempted most; these would undoubtedly be the habitual drunkards, the scandalmongers, the immodest and shameless people who wallow in moral filth, and the miser, who hoards in all sorts of ways. No, my dear brethren, no, it is not these people. On the contrary, the Devil despises them, or else he holds onto them, lest they not have a long enough time in which to do evil, because the longer they live, the more their bad example will drag souls into Hell. Indeed, if the Devil had pursued this lewd and shameless old fellow too closely, he might have shortened the latter's life by fifteen or twenty years, and he would not then have destroyed the virginity of that young girl by plunging her into the unspeakable mire of his indecencies; he would not, again, have seduced that wife, nor would he have taught his evil lessons to that young man, who will perhaps continue to practice them until his death. If the Devil had prompted this thief to rob on every occasion, he would long since have ended on the scaffold and so he would not have induced his neighbor to follow his example. If the Devil had urged this drunkard to fill himself unceasingly with wine, he would long ago have perished in his debaucheries, instead of which, by living longer, he has made many others like himself. If the Devil had taken away the life of this musician, of that dancehall owner, of this cabaret keeper, in some raid or scuffle, or on any other occasion, how many souls would there be who, without these people, would not be damned and who now will be? St. Augustine teaches us that the Devil does not bother these people very much; on the contrary, he despises them and spits upon them.

So, you will ask me, who then are the people most tempted? They are these, my friends; note them carefully. The people most tempted are those who are ready, with the grace of God, to sacrifice everything for the salvation of their poor souls, who renounce all those things which most people eagerly seek. It is not one devil only who tempts them, but millions seek to entrap them. We are told that St. Francis of Assisi and all his religious were gathered on an open plain, where they had built little huts of rushes. Seeing the extraordinary penances which were being practiced, St. Francis ordered that all instruments of penance should be brought out, whereupon his religious produced them in bundles. At this moment there was one young man to whom God gave the grace to see his Guardian Angel. On the one side he saw all of these good religious, who could not satisfy their hunger for penance, and, on the other, his Guardian Angel allowed him to see a gathering of eighteen thousand devils, who were holding counsel to see in what way they could subvert these religious by temptation. One of the devils said: "You do not understand this at all. These religious are so humble; ah, what wonderful virtue, so detached from themselves, so attached to God! They have a superior who leads them so well that it is impossible to succeed in winning them over. Let us wait until their superior is dead, and then we shall try to introduce among them young people without vocations who will bring about a certain slackening of spirit, and in this way we shall gain them."

A little further on, as he entered the town, he saw a devil, sitting by himself beside the gate into the town, whose task was to tempt all of those who were inside. This saint asked his Guardian Angel why it was that in order to tempt this group of religious there had been so many thousands of devils while for a whole town there was but one—and that one sitting down. His good angel told him that the people of the town had not the same need of temptations, that they had enough bad in themselves, while the religious were doing good despite all the traps which the Devil could lay for them.

The first temptation, my dear brethren, which the Devil tries on anyone who has begun to serve God better is in the matter of human respect. He will no longer dare to be seen around; he will hide himself from those with whom heretofore he had been mixing and pleasure seeking. If he should be told that he has changed a lot, he will be ashamed of it! What people are going to say about him is continually in his mind, to the extent that he no longer has enough courage to do good before other people. If the Devil cannot get him back through human respect, he will induce an extraordinary fear to possess him that his confessions are not good, that his confessor does not understand him, that whatever he does will be all in vain, that he will be damned just the same, that he will achieve the same result in the end by letting everything slide as by continuing to fight, because the occasions of sin will prove too many for him.

Why is it, my dear brethren, that when someone gives no thought at all to saving his soul, when he is living in sin, he is not tempted in the slightest, but that as soon as he wants to change his life, in other words, as soon as the desire to give his life to God comes to him, all Hell falls upon him? Listen to what St. Augustine has to say: "Look at the way," he tells us, "in which the Devil behaves towards the sinner. He acts like a jailer who has a great many prisoners locked up in his prison but who, because he has the key in his pocket, is quite happy to leave them, secure in the knowledge that they cannot get out. This is his way of dealing with the sinner who does not consider the possibility of leaving his sin behind. He does not go to the trouble of tempting him. He looks upon this as time wasted because not only is the sinner not thinking of leaving him, but the Devil does not desire to multiply his chains. It would be pointless, therefore, to tempt him. He allows him to live in peace, if, indeed, it is possible to live in peace when one is in sin. He hides his state from the sinner as much as is possible until death, when he then tries to paint a picture of his life so terrifying as to plunge him into despair. But with anyone who has made up his mind to change his life, to give himself up to God, that is another thing altogether."

While St. Augustine lived in sin and evil, he was not aware of anything by which he was tempted. He believed himself to be at peace, as he tells us himself. But from the moment that he desired to turn his back upon the Devil, he had to struggle with him, even to the point of losing his breath in the fight. And that lasted for five years. He wept the most bitter of tears and employed the most austere of penances: "I argued with him," he says, "in my chains. One day I thought myself victorious, the next I was prostrate on the earth again. This cruel and stubborn war went on for five years. However, God gave me the grace to be victorious over my enemy."

You may see, too, the struggle which St. Jerome endured when he desired to give himself to God and when he had the thought of visiting the Holy Land. When he was in Rome, he conceived a new desire to work for his salvation. Leaving Rome, he buried himself in a fearsome desert to give himself over to everything with which his love of God could inspire him. Then the Devil, who foresaw how greatly his conversion would affect others, seemed to burst with fury and despair. There was not a single temptation that he spared him. I do not believe that there is any saint who was as strongly tempted as he. This is how he wrote to one of his friends:

"My dear friend, I wish to confide in you about my affliction and the state to which the Devil seeks to reduce me. How many times in this vast solitude, which the heat of the sun makes insupportable, how many times the pleasures of Rome have come to assail me! The sorrow and the bitterness with which my soul is filled cause me, night and day, to shed floods of tears. I proceed to hide myself in the most isolated places to struggle with my temptations and there to weep for my sins. My body is all disfigured and covered with a rough hair shirt. I have no other bed than the naked ground and my only food is coarse roots and water, even in my illnesses. In spite of all these rigors, my body still experiences thoughts of the squalid pleasures with which Rome is poisoned; my spirit finds itself in the midst of those pleasant companionships in which I so greatly offended God. In this desert to which I have condemned myself to avoid Hell, among these somber rocks, where I have no other companions than the scorpions and the wild beasts, my spirit still burns my body, already dead before myself, with an impure fire; the Devil still dares to offer it pleasures to taste. I behold myself so humiliated by these temptations, the very thought of which makes me die with horror, and not knowing what further austerities I should exert upon my body to attach it to God, that I throw myself on the ground at the foot of my crucifix, bathing it with my tears, and when I can weep no more I pick up stones and beat my breast with them until the blood comes out of my mouth, begging for mercy until the Lord takes pity upon me. Is there anyone who can understand the misery of my state, desiring so ardently to please God and to love Him alone? Yet I see myself constantly prone to offend Him. What sorrow this is for me! Help me, my dear friend, by the aid of your prayers, so that I may be stronger in repelling the Devil, who has sworn my eternal damnation."

These, my dear brethren, are the struggles to which God permits his great saints to be exposed. Alas, how we are to be pitied if we are not fiercely harried by the Devil! According to all appearances, we are the friends of the Devil: he lets us live in a false peace, he lulls us to sleep under the pretense that we have said some good prayers, given some alms, that we have done less harm than others. According to our standard, my dear brethren, if you were to ask, for instance, this pillar of the cabaret if the Devil tempted him, he would answer quite simply that nothing was bothering him at all. Ask this young girl, this daughter of vanity, what her struggles are like, and she will tell you laughingly that she has none at all, that she does not even know what it is to be tempted. There you see, my dear brethren, the most terrifying temptation of all, which is not to be tempted. There you see the state of those whom the Devil is preserving for Hell. If I dared, I would tell you that he takes good care not to tempt or torment such people about their past lives, lest their eyes be opened to their sins.

The greatest of all evils is not to be tempted because there are then grounds for believing that the Devil looks upon us as his property and that he is only awaiting our deaths to drag us into Hell. Nothing could be easier to understand. Just consider the Christian who is trying, even in a small way, to save his soul. Everything around him inclines him to evil; he can hardly lift his eyes without being tempted, in spite of all his prayers and penances. And yet a hardened sinner, who for the past twenty years has been wallowing in sin, will tell you that he is not tempted! So much the worse, my friend, so much the worse! That is precisely what should make you tremble—that you do not know what temptations are. For to say that you are not tempted is like saying the Devil no longer exists or that he has lost all his rage against Christian souls. "If you have no temptations," St. Gregory tells us, "it is because the devils are your friends, your leaders, and your shepherds. And by allowing you to pass your poor life tranquilly, to the end of your days, they will drag you down into the depths." St. Augustine tells us that the greatest temptation is not to have temptations because this means that one is a person who has been rejected, abandoned by God, and left entirely in the grip of one's own passions.

⁊❧ THE BAD DEATH

IF YOU ASK ME WHAT MOST PEOPLE UNDERSTAND by a bad death, I will reply: "When a person dies in the prime of life, married, enjoying good health, having wealth in abundance, and leaves children and a wife desolate, there is no doubt but that such a death is very tragic." King Ezechiel said: "What, my God! It is necessary that I die in the midst of my years, in the prime of my life!" And the Prophet-King asks God not to take him in his prime. Others say that to die at the hands of the executioner on the gallows is a bad death. Others say that a sudden death is a bad death, as, for instance, to be killed in some disaster, or to be drowned, or to fall from a high building and be killed. And then some say that the worst thing is to die of some horrible disease, like the plague or some other contagious malady.

And yet, my dear brethren, I am going to tell you that none of these are bad deaths. Provided that a person has lived well, if he dies in his prime, his death will not fail to be valuable in God's eyes. We have many saints who died in the prime of their lives. It is not a bad death, either, to die at the hands of the executioner. All the martyrs died at the hands of executioners. To die a sudden death is not to die a bad death either, provided one is ready. We have many saints who died deaths of that sort. St. Simeon was killed by lightning on his pillar. St. Francis de Sales died of apoplexy. Finally, to die of the plague is not a dreadful death. St. Roch and St. Francis Xavier died of it.

But what makes death bad is sin. Ah, this horrible sin which tears and devours at this dread moment! Alas, no matter where the poor, unfortunate sinner looks, he sees only sin and neglected graces! If he lifts his eyes to Heaven, he sees only an angry God, armed with all the fury of His justice, Who is ready to punish him. If he turns his gaze downwards, he sees only Hell and its furies already opening its gates to receive him. Alas! This poor sinner did not want to recognize the justice of God during his life on earth; at this moment, not only does he see it, but he feels it already pressing down upon him. During his lifetime, he was always trying to hide his sins, or at least to make as little of them as possible. But at this moment everything is shown to him as in the broad light of day. He sees now what he should have seen before, what he did not want to see. He would like to weep for his sins, but he has no more time. He scorned God during his lifetime; God now, in His turn, scorns him and abandons him to his despair.

Listen, hardened sinners, you who are wallowing now, with such pleasure, in the slime of your vice, without casting even a thought upon amending your lives, who perhaps will give thought to this only when God has abandoned you, as has happened to people less guilty than you. Yes, the Holy Ghost tells us that sinners in their last moments will gnash their teeth, will be seized by a horrible dread, at the very thought of their sins. Their iniquities will rise up before them and accuse them. "Alas!" they will cry at this dread moment, "alas! Of what use is this pride, this vain ostentation, and all those pleasures we have been enjoying in sin? Everything is finished now. We have not a single item of virtue to our credit but have been completely conquered by our evil passions."

This is exactly what happened to the unhappy Antiochus, who, when he fell from his chariot, shattered his whole body. He experienced such dreadful pain in his entrails that it seemed to him as if someone were tearing them out. The worms started to gnaw at him while he was still alive, and his whole body stank like carrion. Then he began to open his eyes. This is what sinners do—but too late.

"Ah," he cried, "I realize now that it was the evils which I committed in Jerusalem that are tormenting me now and gnawing at my heart."

His body was consumed by the most frightful sufferings and his spirit with an inconceivable sadness. He got his friends to come to him, thinking that he might find some consolation in them. But no. Abandoned by God, Who gives consolation, he could not find it in others.

"Alas, my friends," he said to them, "I have fallen into a terrible affliction. Sleep has left me. I cannot rest for a single instant. My heart is pierced with grief. To what a terrible state of sadness and anguish I am reduced! It seems that I must die of sorrow, and in a strange country, too. Ah, Lord, pardon me! I will repair all the evil that I have done. I will pay back all I took from the temple in Jerusalem. I will present great gifts to the temple. I will become a Jew. I will observe the Law of Moses. I will go about publicizing the omnipotence of God. Ah, Lord, have mercy on me, please!"

But his illness increased, and God, Whom he had scorned during his life, no longer had ears to hear him. He was a proud man, a blasphemer, and despite his urgent prayers, he was not listened to and had to go to Hell.

It is a grievous but a just punishment that sinners, who throughout their lives have spurned all the graces which God has offered them, find no more graces when they would like to profit by them. Alas! The number of people who die thus in the sight of God is great. Alas! That there are so many of these blind people who do not open their eyes until the moment when there are no further remedies for their ills!

Yes, my dear brethren, yes, a life of sin and a death of rejection! You are in sin and you do not wish to give it up? No, you say. Very well, my children, you will perish in sin. You will see that in the death of Voltaire, the notorious blasphemer. Listen carefully and you will see that if we despise God always and if God waits for us during our lives, often, by a just judgment, He will abandon us at the hour of our death, when we would like to return to Him.

The idea that one can live in sin and give it all up one day is one of the Devil's traps which will cause you to lose your soul as it has caused so many others to lose theirs. Voltaire, realizing that he was ill, began to reflect upon the state of the sinner who dies with his conscience loaded with sins. He wished to examine his conscience and to see whether God would be willing to pardon him all the sins of his life, which were very great in number. He counted upon the mercy of God, which is infinite, and with this comforting thought in mind, he had brought to him one of those priests whom he had so greatly outraged and calumniated in his writings. He threw himself upon his knees and made a declaration to him of his sins and put into his hands the recantation of all his impieties and his scandals. He began to flatter himself on having achieved the great work of his reconciliation. But he was gravely mistaken. God had abandoned him; you will see how. Death anticipated all spiritual help. Alas! This unfortunate blasphemer felt all his terrors reborn in him. He cried out: "Alas, am I then abandoned by God and men?"

Yes, unhappy man, you are. Already your lot and your hope are in Hell. Listen to this godless man; he cries out with that mouth sullied with so many profanities and so much blasphemy against God, His religion, and His ministers.

"Ah," he cried, "Jesus Christ, Son of God, who died for all sinners without distinction, have pity on me!"

But, alas! Almost a century of blasphemy and impiety had exhausted the patience of God, Who had already rejected him. He was no more than a victim which the wrath of God fattens for the eternal flames. The priests whom he had so derided but whom, in this moment he so desired, were not there. See him as he falls into convulsions and the horrors of despair, his eyes wild, his face ghastly, his body trembling with terror! He twists and turns and torments himself and seems as if he wants to atone for all those previous blasphemies with which his mouth had been so often sullied. His companions in irreligion, fearing, lest someone might bring him the last Sacraments, something which would have seemed to them to dishonor their cause, brought him to a house in the country, and there, abandoned to his despair . . .[9]

ॐ *HIS PRAYER IS A LIE*

I AM SURE YOU WOULD LIKE TO KNOW THE PRAYER of a sinner who neither wants to give up his sin nor is much disturbed by the thought of offending God. Listen: the first word he says as he commences the prayer is a lie. He enters into contradiction with himself. "In the name of the Father and of the Son and of the Holy Ghost." Stop a moment, my friend! You say that you are commencing your prayer in the name of the Three Persons of the Holy Trinity. But surely you must then have forgotten that it is only a week since you were in a crowd where everyone was saying that when one dies, everything is over and that being so, there must be neither God, nor Hell, nor Heaven. If, my dear friend, in your hardness of heart you really believe that, you do not come to pray; you come only to amuse yourself and to pass the time. Ah, you will tell me, those who talk that way are fairly uncommon. Nevertheless, there are some of them among those who are listening to me and yet who do not fail to say some prayers from time to time. Furthermore, I could, if I wished, show you that three-quarters of those who are here in this church, although they do not actually say such things with their lips, say them very often by their conduct and their way of life.

[9] Sermon unfinished.—Trans.

For if a Christian really thinks of what he says when he pronounces the names of the Three Persons of the Holy Trinity, would he not be gripped with a fear which would amount almost to despair when he brought before his mind the image of the Father, which he has defaced in such a shocking way, the image of the Son, which is in his soul, which he has dragged through the slime of his vices, and the image of the Holy Ghost, of whom his heart is the temple and the tabernacle, which he has filled with squalor and obscenity?

Yes, my dear brethren, if the sinner had any knowledge of what he says and what he is, could he pronounce these three names without dying of horror? Listen to this liar: "Oh, my God! I firmly believe that you are here present." Is that so, my friend? Do you really believe that you are in the presence of God, before Whom the angels, who are without stain, tremble and dare not raise their eyes, before Whom they cover themselves with their wings, not being able to withstand the glory of that majesty which Heaven and earth cannot contain? And you, all covered in sins, kneeling there on one knee, do you dare to open your mouth to utter such an abomination? Say, rather, that you are merely imitating, that you are only doing what you see others doing, or, rather, that you are spending a few moments amusing yourself by acting as if you were praying.

❧ HOW BLIND THE SINNER IS!

YOU WILL PROTEST TO ME THAT THIS WAS NOT AT all your intention when you started to pray: "The Lord protect me from committing such a horrible thing!" A nice excuse, my friend! So anyone who commits a sin has no intention of losing grace? Yet he cannot help but lose it. Is he less guilty of the sin? Undoubtedly no, because he knows very well that he cannot do such and such an action, or say such and such a thing, without incurring the guilt of mortal sin. The intention of all the damned who now burn in Hell was certainly not to get themselves damned. Are they the less guilty for all that? No, certainly not, because they knew that they would damn themselves by living the way they lived. A sinner who says his prayers with sin in his heart, without the intention of losing grace, has not the intention of mocking and insulting Jesus Christ. It is none the less true, however, that he does mock Him because he knows well that anyone mocks God when he says to Him: "O my God, I love You," while he loves the sin, or, "I will go to Confession." Listen to that for a lie! He is not even thinking of going to Confession or of being converted from his sin.

But, tell me, what is your intention when you come to church or when you say—as you call it—your prayers? It is, perhaps you will tell me—if you have the hardihood to say it—to perform an act of religion, to give to God the honor and the glory which belong to Him. Oh, horror! Oh, blindness! Oh, impiousness! To wish to honor God by lies—in other words, to want to honor Him by what will outrage Him. Oh, abomination! To have Jesus Christ on your lips and to have Him crucified in your₊ heart! To join what is most holy to what is most detestable, which is the service of the Devil! Oh, what horror! To offer to God a soul which has already been a thousand times prostituted to the Devil! Oh, my God, how blind the sinner is, and all the more blind in that he does not know himself nor even want to know himself!

Was I not right at the beginning to tell you that the prayer of the sinner is nothing other than a tissue of lies and of contradictions? That is so true that the Holy Ghost tells us Himself that the prayer of the sinner who does not wish to renounce his sin is an execration in the eyes of the Lord. You will agree with me that this state is very terrifying and deserving of pity. Very well! Look at how sin blinds one! I say without fear of lying that at least half of those who are listening to me here in this church are in that state. Yet, in fact, is it not true that that does not touch you, but rather that you are bored and that time hangs heavily upon you? You see, my friends, the gloomy abyss to which sin leads a sinner.

To begin with, you know that you have been in sin for six months, or a year, or more, and yet are you not quite contented? Well, yes, you will tell me. That is not difficult to believe, since sin has blurred your vision. You no longer see anything in that state which has hardened your heart so that you no longer feel anything either, and I am just as sure that nothing I have said to you will cause you to think any further about it. Oh, my God, into what depths does sin lead us!

So, you will say, it is of no use saying any more prayers since ours are only insults which we are paying to God. That was not what I wanted you to understand when I told you that your prayers were merely lies. But instead of saying, "My God, I love You," say, "My God, I do not love You, but all I ask is the grace to love You." Instead of saying, "My God, I am very sorry for having offended You," say to Him, "My God, I do not feel any sorrow for my sins, but give me all the sorrow which I ought to have for them." Very far from saying, "My God, I would like to confess my sins," say instead, "My God, I feel myself very much attached to my sins, and it seems to me that I do not want ever to renounce them; give me that horror which I ought to feel for them, so that I may abhor them, detest them, and confess them, so that I may never go back to them!"

O my God, give us, please, that eternal horror of sin, since it is Your enemy, since it was sin that caused Your death, since it robs us of Your friendship, since it separates us from You. O divine Savior, grant that whenever we come to pray, we shall do so with hearts detached from sin, hearts that love You, and hearts that in speaking to You will speak only the truth!

That is the grace, my dear brethren, that I desire for you.

ह PRISONERS OF SIN

IF WE UNDERSTOOD FULLY WHAT IT IS TO RECEIVE the Sacraments, we should bring to the reception of them very much better sentiments than those we do. It is true that the greater number of people, in hiding their sins, always keep at the back of their minds the thought of acknowledging them. Without a miracle, they will not be any the less lost for that. If you want the reason, it is very easy to give it to you. The more we remain in that terrible state which makes Heaven and earth tremble, the more the Devil takes control of us, the more the grace of God diminishes in us, the more our fear increases, the more our sacrileges multiply, and the more we fall away. The result is that we put ourselves almost beyond the possibility of returning into favor with God. I will give you a hundred examples of this against one to the contrary. Tell me, my dear brethren, can you even hope that after passing perhaps five or six years in sacrilege, during which you outraged God more than did all the Jews together, you would dare to believe that God is going to give you all the graces which you will need to emerge from this terrible state? You think that notwithstanding the many crimes against Jesus Christ of which you have been guilty, you have only to say: "I am going to give up sin now and all will be over."

Alas, my friends! Who has guaranteed to you that Jesus Christ will not have made to you the same threat He made to the Jews and pronounce the same sentence which He pronounced against them? . . . You did not wish to profit by the graces which I wanted to give you; but I will leave you alone, and you will seek Me and you will not find Me, and you will die in your sin! . . .

Alas, my dear brethren, our poor souls, once they are in the Devil's hands, will not escape from these as easily as we would like to believe. . . .

Look, my dear brethren, at what the Devil does to mislead us. When we are committing sin, he represents it to us as a mere trifle. He makes us think that there are a great many others who do much worse than we do. Or again, that as we will be confessing the sin, it will be as easy to say four times as twice. But once the sin has been committed, he acts in exactly the opposite way. He represents the sin to us as a monstrous thing. He fills us with such a horror of it that we no longer have the courage to confess it. If we are too frightened to keep the sin hidden, he tells us, to reassure us, that we will confess it at our very next Confession. Subsequently, he tells us that we will not have the courage to do that now, that it would be better to wait for another time to confess it. Take care, my dear brethren; it is only the first step which costs the effort. Once in the prison of the sin, it is very difficult, indeed, to break out of it. . . .

But, you are thinking, I do not really believe that there are many who would be capable of hiding their sins because they would be too much troubled by them. Ah, my dear brethren, if I had to affirm on oath whether there were or were not such people, I would not hesitate to say that there are at least five or six listening to me who are consumed by remorse for their sins and who know that what I say is true. But have patience; you will see them on the day of judgment, and you will recall what I have said to you today. Oh, my God, how shame and fear can hold a Christian soul prisoner in such a terrifying state!

Ah, my dear brethren, what are you preparing for yourselves? You do not dare to make a clean breast of it to your pastor? But is he the only one in the world? Would you not find priests who would have the charity to receive you? Do you think that you would be given too severe a penance? Ah, my children, do not let that stop you! You would be helped; the greater part of it all would be done for you. They would pray for you; they would weep for your sins in order to draw down with greater abundance the mercies of God on you!

My friends, have pity on that poor soul which cost Jesus

Christ so dearly! . . . Oh, my God, who will ever understand the blindness of these poor sinners! You have hidden your sin, my child, but it must be known one day, and then in the eyes of the whole universe, while by one word you would have hidden it forever and you would have changed your hell for an eternity of happiness. Alas, that a sacrilege can lead these poor sinners so far. They do not want to die in that state, but they have not the strength to leave it. My God, torment them so greatly that they will not be able to stay there!

ॐ *YOU CAN BECOME A GOOD TREE*

CONSIDER NOW MY DEAR BRETHREN, THE GOOD works you have done. Have you done them for God alone, so that there was nothing worldly in them and so that you had no regrets when people sometimes proved ungrateful? Have you ever congratulated yourselves inwardly on the good you have done your neighbor? Because if you have done that, either you have done nothing or you may as well count it as nothing, since you have already lost your reward for it. Do you know, my dear brethren, the decision you have to make? If you have done nothing, or if what you have done has been fruitless because it was done for a human motive, begin immediately to do good works so that at death you will be able to find something to offer to Jesus Christ in order that He may give you eternal life.

Perhaps you will say to me: "I have done nothing but evil all my whole life. I am just a bad tree which cannot bring forth good fruit."

My dear brethren, that can very well be, as I am going to show you. Change this tree, moisten it with different water, treat it with some other fertilizer, and you will see that it will bear good fruit, even though it has been bearing bad fruit up to the present. If this tree, which is yourself, has been fruitful in pride, in avarice, in impurity, you can, with the grace of God, see to it that these fruits become abundant in humility, in charity, and in purity. Do yourself as did the earth, which, before the Deluge, drew from its own bosom the water to moisten itself, without having recourse to the clouds of heaven to give it fertility. In the same way, my dear brethren, draw from your own hearts that salutary water which will change your dispositions. You have watered this tree with the foul water of your passions. Well, then, from now on, water it with the tears of repentance, of sorrow, and of love, and you will see that you will cease to be a bad tree and will become one which will bear fruit for life eternal.

To show you, my dear brethren, that this can happen, consider the admirable example furnished in the person of St. Mary Magdalen. Remember how, according to Jesus Christ Himself, she was a bad tree, and then how grace made her into a good tree which brought forth good fruit in abundance. St. Luke tells us that she was a sinner and that she was well known as such in the whole city of Jerusalem. I recommend that you consider what significance those words, which came from the lips of Jesus Christ Himself, have for us. Here was a young girl born with the strongest passions, extraordinary beauty, great wealth—that is to say, with that which not merely kindles the passions but which nourishes and feeds them continually. She was greatly attracted by the pleasures of the world, she had a very strong taste for fashion and a great desire to look beautiful, so that her thoughts and all her cares were employed towards that end. A far from modest air proclaimed openly that her innocence would suffer a speedy shipwreck. Vain and frivolous, the object of admiration by worldlings, she sought all the more to please them, either with provocative glances fired by an impure heart or with her seductive ways and the self-indulgent air which she displayed so brazenly. All of this told a tale of a tree that could only bear plenty of bad fruit.

She received with incredible complaisance the gross glances of the worldlings. She accepted with much self-gratification the silly homage of men. She loved, with more than ordinary enjoyment, to move in the well-to-do social circles of her day. Since she was of great beauty and possessed very considerable wealth, was young and graceful to behold, everyone had, it seemed, eyes and thought for her alone. Dances, spectacles, and the desire to attract and please everyone were all she cared about. If she appeared among the faithful, in the places chosen for prayer, she did so quite eagerly, not to weep for her sins, as she should have been doing, but, rather, to take her place there as the center of attraction that she usually was, to see and—even more—to be seen, and to be admired. Acting thus, it seemed as if she would like to contest with God Himself for men's hearts and the honor which was due Him alone.

She went so far that she finished by becoming a subject of scandal throughout the whole city of Jerusalem. The assignations with the young men, the embraces, the far from modest conversations, the depravities to which she surrendered herself, ended by making her come to be looked upon as a young woman of very evil life. She finished by being avoided and despised by all those of any standing. She was called a sinful and scandalous woman by everyone in the city.

You will admit that here, indeed, was a bad tree. If you have gone as far as she did, there are few who have passed her up. Alas, my friends, what a crop of pride was not borne by that head dressed and ornamented with so much care! What fruits of depravity were not produced in that corrupt heart consumed by an impure fire! And so equally with all the other passions which dominated her. I think, my dear brethren, that it would be difficult to find a more evil tree. Yet, my dear brethren, you shall see that, if we are willing to avail ourselves of the grace which is never lacking to us, any more than it was to Mary Magdalen, miserable though we may be, we can change our tree, which up to now has been bearing only bad fruit. We can make it bear good fruit if we will but make use of the grace which comes to our help. From being bad Christians, we can become good and bear fruit worthy of eternal life, as we shall see by the conversion of Mary Magdalen.

St. Jerome tells us that while Mary Magdalen was thus abandoned to all her passionate and undisciplined ways of living, the stories of so many miracles worked by our Savior in curing the sick and raising the dead to life were filling all Judea with astonishment. Everyone was eager to see so extraordinary a man. Mary Magdalen, happily for herself, was one of this number. The first words which she heard falling from the lips of our Savior were those of the Parables of the Prodigal Son and of the Good Shepherd. She recognized herself exactly in this young man and she also recognized our Savior as the Good Shepherd. The shafts of grace were so lively and so penetrating that she could not help but feel their effects. As the words continued, she felt herself moved to tears. The many miracles that she herself had seen and heard filled her with astonishment, and grace completed the work of changing her, of converting her from a really bad tree into a wonderfully good tree which would bring forth excellent fruit. But what completed the work of detaching her from herself and from sin, the work of breaking through all that held her to these, was the great generosity of God towards sinners. Ah, my dear brethren, how powerful grace is when it finds a heart well disposed! Look at her who began by neither thinking nor acting, but grace pursued her, remorse of conscience tormented her, she felt her heart break with sorrow for her sins. Her eyes, which previously had been so bright with the fire of impurity, which she knew so well how to kindle in the hearts of others, began to shed bitter tears. Since her heart had first tasted the pleasures of the world, she wished it to be the first to feel all the regret for having done evil. From that time, the world of society, which hitherto had held all her pleasure and happiness, could now only weary and disgust her more and more. She discovered that her only happiness lay in being separated from the world and in retirement where she could reflect and shed tears freely.

The more she thought upon the kind of life she had been leading up to then, the outrages she had committed against God, and the number of souls she had lost by her bad life, the more acutely was her heart pierced by sorrow. Such self-love, such proud self-gratification as she had taken in her great beauty, all that worldly homage which had so flattered her—all that now was nothing more to her than a senseless vanity and a kind of idolatry. That vulgar luxury, the worldly amusements which she had always looked upon as the privileges of her age and of her sex, were now in her eyes only a pagan way of living and a real apostasy of her religion. Those passionate sentiments, those indecent liberties, those tender attachments, previously so dear to her heart, and all those mysteries of iniquity, now seemed but crimes and abominations. She realized, as she wept freely and abundantly, that if God had graced her with so many gifts, He had done so but to make her more pleasing to Him. She was therefore the more intensely ashamed of her ingratitude and rebellion.

During these struggles with herself, she learned that a distinguished Pharisee was enjoying the good fortune of entertaining our Savior at his house. She recalled all that she had heard our Lord saying. Yes, she said to herself, I can no longer doubt but that this is the good and charitable Shepherd and that I am but the lost sheep. Ah, she cried, it was I that He meant when He spoke of that prodigal son. So I will rise up and I will go to find Him!

Indeed, unable to contain herself, she started up at once, spurning all her finery and her vanities. She ran, or, rather, the grace with which her heart was already on fire hurried her along. Casting aside all human respect, she entered into the banqueting hall with a downcast air, her hair, previously so beautifully dressed and curled, now quite disheveled, her eyes lowered and bathed in tears, her face blushing and ashamed.

She threw herself at the feet of the Savior, Who was at the table. "Ah, Magdalen, Magdalen!" cries a Father of the Church, "What are you doing and what have you become? Where are all those pleasures, that vanity and that worldly love?" No, no, my dear brethren, here no longer is Magdalen the sinner, but Magdalen the penitent and the faithful lover of our Lord.

Yes, my dear brethren, it was at this moment that everything changed within her. If she had lost so many souls by a life which had been so scandalous, she is now, by her penitent life, going to win even more than those she has lost. She has nothing of human respect left, she accuses herself publicly of her sins before a large assembly, she embraces the feet of our Savior, bathes them with her tears, dries them with her hair. No, no, my dear brethren, Magdalen is no longer Magdalen but a holy lover of God! "No, no, my brethren," St. Augustine says to us, "in Magadalen there is no more vanity, no more pleasure loving, no more worldly love, all is holy and pure in her."

"Yes, my dear brethren," this great saint tells us, "those exquisite perfumes which she had given entirely to luxury, that magnificent head of hair so carefully dressed and ornamented, those beautiful eyes animated with such a dangerous fire, all that is now purified in her tears."

"Ah! my dear brethren," he says to us, "who could tell us what passes in her heart? Everyone of those who were witnesses of this generous gesture turns it into ridicule, treats her as deranged, blames and condemns her, except Jesus Christ Himself, Who knows so well that it is His grace which has done all for her."

He is so touched by it that He says nothing to her of her sins. But He takes a particular pleasure in praising her for the kindness she has done to Him, and that in front of all the assembled guests: "Go in peace," He said to her tenderly, "thy sins are forgiven thee."

Since your soul is as precious in God's eyes as that of Mary Magdalen's, you can be quite sure, my dear brethren, that grace will never be wanting to you to convert you and to help you to persevere.

ࢶ *WHERE ARE YOU GOING?*

AH, WHO WOULD NOT BE TOUCHED? . . . A GOD WHO weeps with so many tears at the loss of one soul and Who cries unceasingly: My friend, my friend, why proceedest thou thus to lose thy soul and thy God? Stop! Stop! Ah! Look at my tears, my Blood which flows yet. Must I die a second time to save thee? Look at me. Ah! Angels from Heaven descend upon earth, come and weep with me for the loss of this soul!

Oh, that a Christian should be so unfortunate as to persevere still in running towards the abyss despite the voice which his God causes him to hear continually!

But, you may say to me, no one says these things to us. Oh my friends, unless you want to stop up your ears, you will hear the voice of God, which follows you unceasingly. Tell me, my friends, then, what is this remorse of conscience which overwhelms you in the midst of sin? Why do these anxieties and storms agitate you? Why this fear, this dread that you are in, when you seem to be forever expecting to be crushed by the thunders of Heaven? How many times, even when you were sinning, have you not experienced the touch of an invisible hand which seemed to push you away, as if someone were saying: Unhappy man, what are you doing? Unhappy man, where are you going? Ah my son, why do you wish to damn yourself? . . .

Would you not agree with me that a Christian who despises so many graces deserves to be abandoned and rejected because he has not listened to the voice of God or profited by His graces? On the contrary, my dear brethren, it is God Himself Who is scorned by this ungrateful soul who would seem to wish to put Him to death again. All creation demands vengeance, and it is, in fact, God alone Who wishes to save this soul and Who is opposed to all that could be prejudicial to it. He watches over its salvation as if it were the only soul in the world.

⇨ *ANNUAL CONFESSIONS*

If EASTER WERE PROLONGED TO PENTECOST, YOU would not go to Confession until Pentecost, or if the latter did not come around for ten years, you would go to Confession only every ten years. Indeed, if the Church did not give you a commandment about it, you would not go to Confession until death. What do you think of that, my dear brethren? Does it not mean that you have neither regret for having offended God, Who requires you to go to Confession, nor love for God, Who requires you to make your Easter Communion?

Ah you will say to me, that's all very well. We do not make our Easter duty without knowing why.

Ah! You know nothing at all about it! You do it from habit, to be able to say you have made your Easter duty, or, if you would prefer to speak the truth, you would say that you have added a new sin to your old ones. It is not, therefore, either love of God or regret for having offended Him which makes you go to Confession or make your Easter duty, or even the desire to lead a more Christian life. And here is the proof of it: if you loved God, would you consent to commit sin with such ease, and even with so much enjoyment? If you had a horror of sin, as you should have, would you be able to keep it for a whole year on your conscience? If you had a real desire to live a more Christian life, would we not see at least some little change in your way of living?

No, my dear brethren, I do not wish to talk to you today about those unfortunate people who tell only half their sins through fear of not making their Easter duty or of being refused Absolution—perhaps even for the sake of covering up their shameful lives with the veil of virtue and who, in this state, approach the altar and are going to complete their dreadful work by handing over their God to the Devil and precipitating their sacrilegious souls into Hell.

No, I dare to hope that this does not concern you, but I will continue, nevertheless, to tell you that going to Confession only once a year is not something about which you should feel any peace or satisfaction.

?~ *THOUGHTS ABOUT PENANCE*

TELL ME, MY DEAR BRETHREN, WHAT ARE THE penances that are given to you? Alas! A few rosaries, some litanies, some almsgivings, a few little mortifications. Do all of these things, I ask you, bear any proportion to our sins which deserve eternal punishment? There are some who carry out their penance walking along or sitting down; that is not doing it at all. Unless the priest tells you that you may do it while walking along or sitting down, you should do your penance on your knees. If you do perform your penance while walking along or sitting down, you should confess it and never do it again.

In the second place, unless you are not able to do it as required, in which event you must tell that to your confessor when you go to Confession the next time, I must tell you that the penance should be done within the time indicated; otherwise you commit a sin. For example, the priest might tell you to make a visit to the Blessed Sacrament after the services because he knows that you go around in company which will not bring you any nearer to God; he may order you to mortify yourself in something which you eat because you are subject to gluttony; to make an act of contrition if you have the misfortune to fall back into the sin which you have just confessed. At other times you may wait until the moment when you are ready to go to Confession to do your penance. You understand as well as I do that in all of these instances you are fully at fault and that you should not fail to confess that and that you should never do this again.

In the third place, I tell you that you should perform your penance devoutly, that is to say, with reverence and with the sincere intention of giving up the sin. To say your penance reverently, my dear brethren, is to say it with attention to its spiritual importance and with devotion in your hearts. If you have said your penance with willful distractions, you will not have said it at all, and you are obliged to say it again. To perform it devoutly is to perform it with a strong confidence that God will forgive you your sins through the merits of Jesus Christ, Who made satisfaction for us by His sufferings and His death on the Cross. We should perform our penance overwhelmed with joy at being able to satisfy God, Whom we have offended, and at finding such an easy means of effacing our sins which should have earned eternal sufferings for us. Something which you should never forget is that all the time you are fulfilling your penance, you should be saying to God: "My God, I unite this slight penance to that which Jesus Christ my Savior has offered to You for my sins." This is what will make your penance meritorious and pleasing to God. I repeat that we should always carry out our penance with the true desire to give up the sin altogether, no matter what it may cost us, even if it involves death itself. If we have not these dispositions, very far from satisfying the justice of God, we will outrage it again, which would make us even more guilty.

I have said that we should never content ourselves with the penance which our confessor imposes upon us because it is nothing, or almost nothing, if we compare it with what our sins really deserve. If our confessor is so very lenient with us, it is only lest he might give us a distaste for the work of our salvation. If you really have your salvation at heart, you should impose penances upon yourself.

Choose those which suit your case best. If you have the misfortune to be someone who gives scandal, you should make yourself so watchful of your behavior that your neighbor will not be able to see anything in your life which would give him anything but good example; you should show by your conduct that your life is truly Christian. If you are one of those unhappy people who sin against the holy virtue of purity, you should mortify that sinful body with fasting, giving it only what it needs to sustain life and to fulfill its functions, from time to time making it sleep upon bare boards. If you are one of those who has to have something to eat which will gratify your gluttony, you should refuse this to your body and despise it as much as you previously loved it. When your body wants to cost you your soul, you must punish it. Your heart, which must often have thought of impure things, has carried your thoughts into Hell, which is the place reserved for the unchaste. If you are attached to the things of this earth, you should give alms sufficient to enable you to punish your avarice by depriving yourself of all that is not absolutely necessary for life.

If we have been negligent in the service of God, let us impose upon ourselves the penance of assisting at all the exercises of piety which are going on in our parish. I would advise Mass, Vespers, catechism, prayers, the Rosary, so that God, seeing our eagerness, may be good enough to pardon us all our negligences. If we have spare time between the services, let us do some spiritual reading, which will nourish our souls—above all, some reading of the lives of the saints wherein we may see how they behaved in order to sanctify themselves. That will encourage us. Let us make some short visit to the Blessed Sacrament during the week to ask God to pardon the sins we have committed. If we feel ourselves guilty of some fault, let us go and get rid of it so that our prayers and all our good works may be pleasing to God and more advantageous to our souls. Have we the habit of swearing or of flying into rages? Let us go down on our knees to say again this holy prayer: "My God, may your holy name be blessed for ever and ever! My God, purify my heart, purify my lips so that they may never pronounce words which would outrage you and separate me from you!" Any time that you fall into this sin, you should immediately either make an act of contrition or give away something to the poor. Have you been working on Sunday? Have you been buying or selling without necessity in the course of this holy day? Give to the poor some alms which will exceed the profit you have made. Have you been eating or drinking to excess? In all your meals you should deprive yourself of something.

Such, my dear brethren, are the penances which will not only suffice to make satisfaction to the justice of God, if joined to those of Jesus Christ, but which can even preserve you from falling again into your sins. If you want to conduct yourselves in this way, you will be sure, with the grace of God, of correcting your faults.

ᕲᕽ REPAIRING THE WRONG DONE

HAVING MADE SATISFACTION TO GOD, WE MUST then make satisfaction to our neighbor for the wrong which—either in his body or in his soul—we have done him. I say that it is possible to wrong him in his body, that is to say, in his person, by attacking him either by injurious or insulting words or by bad treatment. If we have sinned against him by injurious words, then we must apologize to him and make our reconciliation with him. If we have done him some wrong by belaboring his animals, as sometimes happens when we find that they have been doing damage among our crops, we are obliged to give him all that we have been the cause of his losing: we could have got compensation without maltreating these animals. If we have done any harm, we are obliged to repay as soon as we can;

otherwise we will be gravely at fault. If we have neglected to do that, we have sinned and we must confess it.

If you have done wrong to your neighbor in his honor, as, for instance, by scandalous talk, you are obliged to make up by favorable and beneficent talk for all the harm you have done to his reputation, saying all the good of him which you know to be true and concealing any faults which he may have and which you are not obliged to reveal. If you have calumniated your neighbor, you must go and find the people to whom you have said false things about him and tell them that what you have been saying is not true, that you are very grieved about it, and that you beg them not to believe it.

But if you have done him harm in his soul, it is a still more difficult thing to repair, and yet it must be done as far as possible; otherwise God will not pardon you.

You must also examine your conscience as to whether you have given scandal to your children or to your next-door neighbors. How many fathers, mothers, masters, and mistresses are there who scandalize their children and their servants by not saying their prayers morning or evening or by saying them when they are dressing or sitting back in a chair, who do not even make the Sign of the Cross before and after a meal? How many times are they heard swearing, or perhaps even blaspheming? How many times have they been seen working on Sunday morning, even before Holy Mass?

You must consider, too, whether you have sung bad songs, or brought in bad books, or whether you have given bad counsel, as, for instance, advising someone that he should take his revenge on someone else, should exact satisfaction by force. Consider, too, whether you have ever taken anything from a next-door neighbor and neglected to pay it back, whether you have neglected to give some alms which you had been told to give or make some restitution which your parents, who are dead, should have made. If you wish to have the happiness of having your sins forgiven, you must have nothing belonging

to anyone else which you should and could pay back. So if
you have sullied your neighbor's reputation, you must do all
in your power to repair the damage. You must be reconciled
with your enemies, speak to them as if they had never done
you anything but good all your life, keeping nothing in your
heart but the charity which the good Christian should have for
everyone, so that we can all appear with confidence before the
tribunal of God. That is the happiness that....[10]

ཧྥ RENOUNCE SIN FOR GOOD AND ALL

ALL THAT IS VERY TRUE, YOU WILL TELL ME, BUT
what will people say about me after seeing me go to Confession
several times and then not make my Easter duty? People are
going to believe that I am leading a bad life; besides, I know
plenty of others who are worse sinners than I who have been
given absolution; you have received So-and-So well, and he has
broken the law of abstinence with me; and So-and-So, who has
been out on Sundays, as well as I have, at....[11]

The conscience of another person is not yours. If he does
wrong, it is not for you to listen to accounts of it. Or do you
want, just in order to keep up appearances, to damn your soul
by committing sacrilege? Would not that be the greatest of all
evils? You think that people will notice you because they have
seen you going to Confession several times and yet you have
not been to Holy Communion. Ah, my poor friend, fear rather
the eyes of God, before which you have done the wrong, and
pay no attention to all the others. You say that you know of
some, more guilty than you, who have been given Absolution.
What do you know of them? Did an angel come to you to tell

[10] Sentence incomplete.—Trans.
[11] Sentence incomplete.—Trans.

you that God had not changed or converted them? And even if they should not have been converted, should you therefore do wrong because they do wrong? Would you want to be damned because others are damning themselves? Dear God, what frightful talk!

But, these penitents still protest, these penitents who not only have not been converted, but who indeed do not want to be converted at all but only to save their faces in public. . . . When will it be the right time then to come for Holy Communion?

When will it be time to come for Holy Communion? Listen to St. John Chrysostom. He himself is going to tell us when it will be time for Holy Communion. Is it at Easter, at Pentecost, at Christmas? No, he tells us. Is it at the point of death? No, he tells us again. When is it then? It is, he says to us, when we have renounced sin for good and all, and are fully resolved, with the help of God's grace, not to fall into it again. When you have paid back that which is not yours, when you have become reconciled with your enemy—that is when you are genuinely converted.

Other sinners will tell us: "If you are going to be so difficult, we will go to those who will allow us to go to Holy Communion. Look at how many times I have come. I have other things to do than to be walking the roads. I am not coming back for a long time, for I can see quite plainly that you are angry with me. What great harm have I done, then?"

You will go to find another, my friend? You are entirely free to go to anyone who seems good to you. But do you think that another would wish, any more than I would, to damn himself? No, I am sure you do not. If he receives you, it is because he does not know you well enough. Do you want to know what sort of a person talks like that, and who goes in search of Absolution elsewhere? Listen, and tremble. He leaves his guide, who can lead him surely, to look for a passport to go straight to Hell.

But, you will say to me, look at how many times I keep coming.

Very well, my friend! Change your ways and you will be allowed Absolution the very first time you return.

I am not coming back, you say, for a very long time.

So much the worse for you alone, my poor friend. In not coming back you are taking a big step in the direction of Hell. There are some who are so blind that they will go so far as to believe that the confessor is angry with them because he does not give them Absolution. Undoubtedly, my friends, he is vexed with you, but it is because he desires the salvation of your poor souls. It is for that reason that he does not want to give you an Absolution which, very far from saving you, would damn you for all eternity.

But, you say, what have I done that is so bad? I have not killed, or stolen. . . .

You say not killed, not stolen, you say? But, my friend, Hell is full of other people who have not killed or stolen. There are more than two sins which drag souls into Hell. But if we were so lax as to give you Absolution when you do not merit it, we would be playing the part of executioner of your poor soul, which caused so much suffering to Jesus Christ.

৯৯ *MERIT ABSOLUTION*

WHEN ANYONE HAS REALLY GIVEN UP HIS SINS, HE must not be content simply with bewailing them. He must also give up, leave far behind, and fly from anything which is capable of leading him in the direction of them again. In other words, my dear brethren, we must be ready to suffer anything rather than fall back into those sins which we have just confessed. People should be able to see a complete change in us; otherwise we have not merited Absolution, and it could even be possible that we have indeed committed sacrilege. Alas, that there are few in whom this change is apparent after having received Absolution! . . . Dear God, what sacrileges are committed! . . . If in every thirty Absolutions there were but one genuine case, how soon would the world be converted!

Those people do not merit Absolution, then, who do not give sufficient signs of contrition. Alas, how many times, because they are sent away, do they not come back any more! This, of course, is because they have no real urge to be converted, for if they truly had, very far from leaving their Confession until another Easter, they would be working with all their hearts to change their lives and to return to make their peace with God.

ॐ *PRAYER COMMANDS ALL*

MY DEAR BRETHREN, NOT ONLY IS PRAYER VERY efficacious, but, even more, it is of the utmost necessity for overcoming the enemies of our salvation. Look at all the saints: they were not content with watching and fighting to overcome the enemies of their salvation and with keeping well away from all that could offer temptation to them. They passed their whole lives in prayer, not only the day, but very often the whole night. Yes, my dear children, we will watch over ourselves and all the motions of our hearts in vain, in vain we will avoid temptation if we do not pray; if we do not have continual recourse to prayer, all our other ways will be of no use at all to us and we shall be overcome. We can see plainly that in the world there are a great many occasions when we cannot run away; for example, a child cannot run away from the society of his parents because of their bad example. But he can pray, and his prayer will sustain him.

Even supposing that we could run away from people who give us bad example, we cannot run away from ourselves, who are our biggest enemy. If our Lord does not watch over our preservation, all of our efforts will come to nothing. No, my children, we shall not find any sinner who may be converted who has not recourse to prayer, not one who will persevere without having very great recourse to prayer, and we shall never find a Christian damned whose downfall did not commence with a lack of prayer. We can see too how much the Devil fears those who pray, since there is no moment of the day when he tempts us more than at prayer. He does everything he possibly can to prevent us from praying. When the Devil wants to make someone lose his soul, he starts out by inspiring in him a profound distaste for prayer. However good a Christian he may be, if the Devil succeeds in making him either say his prayers badly or neglect them altogether, he is certain to have him for himself. If you wish to understand this even better, consider since when you have been unable to resist whatever temptations the Devil put in your way and since when you have left the door of your hearts open to the four winds—is it not since you began to get careless with your prayers, or have been saying them from habit, by routine only, or just to get rid of them, and not to please God? Yes, my dear brethren, from the moment that we neglect them, we move with big steps towards Hell: we shall never return to God if we do not have recourse to prayer. Yes, my dear children, with a prayer well said, we can command Heaven and earth, and all will obey us.

๛ *YOU HAVE NOT THE TIME*

WE CAN ONLY FIND OUR HAPPINESS ON EARTH IN loving God, and we can only love Him in prayer to Him. We see that Jesus Christ, to encourage us often to have recourse to Him through prayer, promises never to refuse us anything if we pray for it as we should. But there is no need to go looking for elaborate and roundabout ways of showing you that we should pray often, for you have only to open your catechism and you will see there that the duty of every good Christian is to pray morning and evening and often during the day—that is to say, always. . . .

Which of us, my dear brethren, could, without tears of compassion, listen to those poor Christians who dare to say that they have not time to pray? You have not the time! Poor blind creatures, which is the more precious action: to strive to please God and to save your soul, or to go out to feed your animals in the stable or to call your children or your servants in order to send them out to till the earth or to tidy up the stable? Dear God! How blind man is! . . . You have not the time! But tell me, ungrateful creatures, if God had called you to die that night, would you have exerted yourselves? If He had sent you three or four months of illness, would you have exerted yourselves? Go away, you miserable creatures; you deserve to have God abandon you in your blindness and leave you thus to perish. We find that it is too much to give Him a few minutes to thank Him for the graces which He is giving us at every instant! . . .

You must get on with your work, you say.

That, my dear people, is where you are greatly mistaken. You have no other work to do except to please God and to save your souls. All the rest is not your work. If you do not do it, others will, but if you lose your soul, who will save it?

ಶಿ *I COME ON BEHALF OF GOD*

WHY AM I UP IN THE PULPIT TODAY, MY DEAR brethren? What am I going to say to you? Ah! I come on behalf of God Himself. I come on behalf of your poor parents, to awaken in you that love and gratitude which you owe them. I come to bring before your minds again all those kindnesses and all the love which they gave you while they were on earth. I come to tell you that they suffer in Purgatory, that they weep, and that they demand with urgent cries the help of your prayers and your good works. I seem to hear them crying from the depths of those fires which devour them: "Tell our loved ones, tell our children, tell all our relatives how great the evils are which they are making us suffer. We throw ourselves at their feet to implore the help of their prayers. Ah! Tell them that since we have been separated from them, we have been here burning in the flames! Oh! Who would be so indifferent to such sufferings as we are enduring?"

Do you see, my dear brethren, do you hear that tender mother, that devoted father, and all those relatives who helped and tended you? "My friends," they cry, "free us from these pains; you can do it." Consider then, my dear brethren: (1) the magnitude of these sufferings which the souls in Purgatory endure; and (2) the means which we have of mitigating them: our prayers, our good works, and, above all, the holy sacrifice of the Mass.

I do not wish to stop at this stage to prove to you the existence of Purgatory. That would be a waste of time. No one among you has the slightest doubt on that score. The Church, to which Jesus Christ promised the guidance of the Holy Ghost and which, consequently, can neither be mistaken herself nor mislead us, teaches us about Purgatory in a very clear and positive manner. It is certain, very certain, that there is a place where the souls of the just complete the expiation of their sins before being admitted to the glory of Paradise, which is assured them. Yes, my dear brethren, and it is an article of faith: if we have not done penance proportionate to the greatness and enormity of our sins, even though forgiven in the holy tribunal of Penance, we shall be compelled to expiate them. . . . In Holy Scripture there are many texts which show clearly that although our sins may be forgiven, God still imposes on us the obligation to suffer in this world by temporal hardships or in the next by the flames of Purgatory.

Look at what happened to Adam. Because he was repentant

after committing his sin, God assured him that He had pardoned him, and yet He condemned him to do penance for nine hundred years, penance which surpasses anything that we can imagine. See again: David ordered, contrary to the wish of God, the census of his subjects, but, stricken with remorse of conscience, he recognized his sin and, throwing himself upon the ground, begged the Lord to pardon him. God, touched by his repentance, forgave him indeed. But despite that, He sent Gad to tell David that he would have to choose between three scourges which He had prepared for him as punishment for his iniquity: the plague, war, or famine. David said: "It is better that I should fall into the hands of the Lord (for his mercies are many) than into the hands of men." He chose the pestilence, which lasted three days and killed seventy thousand of his subjects. If the Lord had not stayed the hand of the Angel, which was stretched out over the city, all Jerusalem would have been depopulated! David, seeing so many evils caused by his sin, begged the grace of God to punish him alone and to spare his people, who were innocent.[12]

Alas, my dear brethren, what, then, will be the number of years which we shall have to suffer in Purgatory, we who have so many sins, we who, under the pretext that we have confessed them, do no penance and shed no tears? How many years of suffering shall we have to expect in the next life?

But how, when the holy Fathers tell us that the torments they suffer in this place seem to equal the sufferings which our Lord Jesus Christ endured during His sorrowful Passion, shall I paint for you a heart-rending picture of the sufferings which these poor souls endure? However, it is certain that if the slightest torment that our Lord suffered had been shared by all mankind, they would all be dead through the violence of such suffering. The fire of Purgatory is the same as the fire of Hell; the difference between them is that the fire of Purgatory is not ever-

[12] "See, too, the penance of St. Mary Magdalen; perhaps that will soften your hearts a little." (Note by the Curé of Ars)

lasting. Oh! Should God in His great mercy permit one of these poor souls, who burn in these flames, to appear here in my place, all surrounded by the fires which consume him, and should he give you himself a recital of the sufferings he is enduring, this church, my dear brethren, would reverberate with his cries and his sobs, and perhaps that might finally soften your hearts.

Oh! How we suffer! they cry to us. Oh! You, our brethren, deliver us from these torments! You can do it! Ah, if you only experienced the sorrow of being separated from God! . . . Cruel separation! To burn in the fire kindled by the justice of God! . . . To suffer sorrows incomprehensible to mortal man! . . . To be devoured by regret, knowing that we could so easily have avoided such sorrows! . . . Oh! My children, cry the fathers and the mothers, can you thus so readily abandon us, we who loved you so much? Can you then sleep in comfort and leave us stretched upon a bed of fire. Will you have the courage to give yourselves up to pleasure and joy while we are here suffering and weeping night and day? You have our wealth, our homes, you are enjoying the fruit of our labors, and you abandon us here in this place of torments, where we are suffering such frightful evils for so many years! . . . And not a single almsgiving, not a single Mass which would help to deliver us! . . . You can relieve our sufferings, you can open our prison, and you abandon us. Oh! How cruel these sufferings are! . . .

Yes, my dear brethren, people judge very differently, when in the flames of Purgatory, of all those light faults, if indeed it is possible to call anything light which makes us endure such rigorous sorrows. What woe would there be to man, the Royal Prophet cries, even the most just of men, if God were to judge him without mercy. If God has found spots in the sun and malice in the angels, what, then, is this sinful man? And for us, who have committed so many mortal sins and who have done practically nothing to satisfy the justice of God, how many years of Purgatory! . . .

"My God," said St. Teresa, "what soul will be pure enough

to enter into heaven without passing through the vengeful flames?" In her last illness, she cried suddenly: "O justice and power of my God, how terrible you are!" During her agony, God allowed her to see His holiness as the angels and the saints see Him in heaven, which caused her so much dread that her sisters, seeing her trembling and extraordinarily agitated, spoke to her, weeping: "Ah! Mother, what has happened to you; surely you do not fear death after so many penances and such abundant and bitter tears?"

"No, my children," St. Teresa replied, "I do not fear death; on the contrary, I desire it so that I may be united forever with my God."

"Is it your sins, then, which terrify you, after so much mortification?"

"Yes, my children," she told them. "I do fear my sins, but I fear still another thing even more."

"Is it the judgment then?"

"Yes, I tremble at the formidable account that it will be necessary to render to God, Who, in that moment, will be without mercy, but there is still something else of which the very thought alone makes me die with terror."

The poor sisters were deeply distressed.

"Alas! Can it be Hell then?"

"No," she told them. "Hell, thank God, is not for me. Oh! My sisters, it is the holiness of God. My God, have pity upon me! My life must be brought face to face with that of Jesus Christ Himself! Woe to me if I have the least blemish or stain! Woe to me if I am even in the very shadow of sin!"

"Alas!" cried these poor sisters. "What will our deaths be like!"

What will ours be like, then, my dear brethren, we who, perhaps in all our penances and our good works, have never yet satisfied for one single sin forgiven in the tribunal of Penance? Ah! What years and centuries of torment to punish us! . . . How dearly we shall pay for all those faults that we look upon as nothing at all, like those little lies that we tell to amuse ourselves, those little scandals, the despising of the graces which God gives us at every moment, those little murmurings in the difficulties that He sends us! No, my dear brethren, we would never have the courage to commit the least sin if we could understand how much it outrages God and how greatly it deserves to be rigorously punished, even in this world.

God is just, my dear brethren, in all that He does. When He recompenses us for the smallest good action, He does so over and above all that we could desire. A good thought, a good desire, that is to say, the desire to do some good work even when we are not able to do it, He never leaves without a reward. But also, when it is a matter of punishing us, it is done with rigor, and though we should have only a light fault, we shall be sent into Purgatory. This is true, for we see it in the lives of the saints that many of them did not go to Heaven without having first passed through the flames of Purgatory. St. Peter Damien tells that his sister remained several years in Purgatory because she had listened to an evil song with some little pleasure. It is told that two religious promised each other that the first to die would come to tell the survivor in what state he was. God permitted the one who died first to appear to his friend. He told him that he was remaining fifteen years in Purgatory for having liked to have his own way too much. And as his friend was complimenting him on remaining there for so short a time, the dead man replied: "I would have much preferred to be flayed alive for ten thousand years continuously, for that suffering could not even be compared with what I am suffering in the flames."

A priest told one of his friends that God had condemned him to remain in Purgatory for several months for having held back the execution of a will designed for the doing of good works. Alas, my dear brethren, how many among those who hear me have a similar fault with which to reproach themselves? How many are there, perhaps, who during the course of eight or ten years have received from their parents or their friends the work of having Masses said and alms given and have allowed the whole thing to slide! How many are there who, for fear of finding that certain good works should be done, have not wanted to go to the trouble of looking at the will that their parents or their friends have made in their favor? Alas, these poor souls are still detained in the flames because no one has desired to fulfill their last wishes! Poor fathers and mothers, you are being sacrificed for the happiness of your children and your heirs! You perhaps have neglected your own salvation to augment their fortune. You are being cheated of the good works which you left behind in your wills! . . . Poor parents! How blind you were to forget yourselves! . . .

You will tell me, perhaps: "Our parents lived good lives; they were very good people." Ah! They needed little to go into these flames! See what Albert the Great, a man whose virtues shone in such an extraordinary way, said on this matter. He revealed one day to one of his friends that God had taken him into Purgatory for having entertained a slightly self-satisfied thought about his own knowledge. The most astonishing thing was that there were actually saints there, even ones who were canonized, who were passing through Purgatory. St. Séverinus, Archbishop of Cologne, appeared to one of his friends a long time after his death and told him that he had been in Purgatory for having deferred to the evening the prayers he should have said in the morning. Oh! What years of Purgatory will there be for those Christians who have no difficulty at all in deferring their prayers to another time on the excuse of having to do some pressing work! If we really desired the happiness of possessing God, we should avoid the little faults as well as the big ones, since separation from God is so frightful a torment to all these poor souls!

ဒ YOU SHOULD COME EARLIER

DO YOU WANT TO KNOW, MY DEAR BRETHREN, HOW we should conduct ourselves when we want to have the happiness of receiving God? Do as that good Christian does who goes to Holy Communion every week. He uses three of the days in thanksgiving and three in preparation. Well, who is stopping you from making all of your actions preparations for this? During this time, maintain an intercourse with Jesus Christ, Who reigns in your heart, so that He may visit your soul and enrich it with all kinds of blessings and happiness. You should implore the Blessed Virgin, the angels, and the saints to pray to God for you that you may receive Him as worthily as is possible. On the day itself, you should come earlier to the holy Mass and follow it even more closely than at other times.

Your mind and your heart should be continuously at the foot of the tabernacle, they should yearn unceasingly for this happy moment, and you yourself should be so plunged into the depths of the very thought of God that you should seem to be dead to the world. You should have your prayer book or your rosary beads with you, and you should say your Acts with as much fervor as you possibly can in order to rekindle in yourself faith, hope, and a great love for Jesus Christ, Who is coming in a moment to make your heart His tabernacle, or, if you like, a little Heaven. Dear God! What happiness and what honor for miserable creatures like us! We should express a great respect to Him. So miserable a being! . . . But we hope that He will have pity on us all the same.

After having said your Acts, you should offer your Holy Communion for yourself and for others. You should get up to approach the altar with all possible modesty, which shows that you are about to do something very great. You kneel down and you make the effort to rekindle in yourself the faith which will make you realize the greatness of your happiness. Your mind and your heart must be absolutely on God. You must take good care not to turn your head, you keep your eyes partially closed, your hands joined, and you say your "I confess to God." If you are waiting for Holy Communion, you should excite a very fervent love for Jesus Christ and pray very humbly that He will deign to come into your poor and miserable heart.

After you have had the wonderful happiness of receiving Holy Communion, you should rise with modesty and return to your place. You should stay a moment with our Lord Jesus Christ, Whom you have the joy of having in your heart, where, for a quarter of an hour, He is present in both Body and Soul as during His mortal life. Oh, infinite happiness! Who will ever understand it! Alas! Hardly anyone understands it! After you have asked God for all the graces you desire for yourself and others, you should then take up your prayer book again and continue to use it. After saying your Acts after Holy Communion, you should invite the Blessed Virgin and all the angels and saints to thank God for you. You should be careful not to spit, at least for a good half-hour, after receiving Holy Communion. Do not go out immediately after holy Mass but stay a moment to ask God to give you plenty of strength to keep to your good resolutions. When you go out of the church, do not delay to chat. You should think about the great joy you have had in receiving Jesus Christ and make your way home.

If you have a moment to spare between the services, you should employ it in some spiritual reading or in making a visit to the Blessed Sacrament to thank God for the grace He gave you in the morning, and you should think about worldly matters as little as possible. You should so watch over all your thoughts, your words, and your actions that you may keep the grace of God all your life.

ࣻ *IT IS NECESSARY TO BE CONVERTED*

No, MY DEAR BRETHREN, LET US NEVER FORGET that in order to receive Holy Communion it is necessary to be converted and strong in a true resolution to persevere. When Jesus Christ desired to give His Adorable Body and His Precious Blood to His Apostles, in order to teach them how pure one should be before receiving It, He even went so far as to wash their feet. By that He wishes to show us that we can never be purified enough of our sins, even our venial sins. It is true that the venial sin does not make our Communions unworthy, but it is a cause of our profiting hardly at all by such a great blessing and happiness. The proof of that is very clear when you consider how many times we have received Holy Communion during the course of our lives. And have we become any better? . . . No, not at all, and the real cause of that is that practically all the time we are holding onto our bad habits; we do not break ourselves of any one of them more than another. We have a horror of the big sins which kill our souls, but all those little fits of impatience, those grumblings when some worries or troubles befall us, or some disappointments or setbacks—these mean nothing to us. You will admit that in spite of so many Confessions and Holy Communions, you are always the same, that your Confessions are nothing else, nor have they been for years, than a repetition of the same sins, which, although venial, are none the less damaging to the merit of your Holy Communions. You have been heard to say, with good reason, that you are no better one day than another, but who is stopping you from correcting your faults? . . . If you are always the same, it is simply because you do not want to make even small efforts to improve yourself. You do not want to endure anything or to be opposed in anything. You would like everyone to be fond of you and to have a good opinion of you, which is a difficult enough thing.

Let us try hard, my dear brethren, to destroy all that could be in the smallest way displeasing to Jesus Christ, and we shall see how our Communions will help us to make great strides towards Heaven. And the more we do this, the more we shall feel ourselves becoming detached from sin and inclining towards God. . . . This is what I desire for you.

ॐ *HAVE A CLEAN FACE*

I HAVE TOLD YOU THAT YOU SHOULD HAVE NEAT and clean clothes. I do not mean expensive clothes, but only ones which are not soiled or torn. That is to say, the clothes should be washed and mended if one has no others. There are some who have nothing to change or who, through laziness, do not do so; they do not change their linen, that is, their shirts. For those who have no other clothes, there is nothing wrong in that. But those who have, do wrong, for it is lacking in respect to our Lord, Who wishes to come into their hearts. Your hair should be combed and tidy and your face and hands clean. You should never come to the altar without stockings, good or bad. One should not approve of those young people who, in going up to the altar, appear no differently at that moment than at the time when they are going to a ball or a dance. I do not know how they go to receive a God Who was humbled and despised by all, with such a parade of vanity and style. Dear Lord, what a contradiction this is! . . .

ॐ *MODEL YOUR DEATH UPON THAT OF JESUS CHRIST*

IF WE WERE REQUIRED TO DIE TWICE, WE COULD jettison one death. But man dies once only, and upon his death depends his eternity. Where the tree falls, there shall it lie. If, at the hour of his death, someone is living in some bad habit, his poor soul will fall on the side of Hell. If, on the other hand, he is in the state of grace, it will take the road for heaven. Oh, happy road! . . .

Generally speaking, one dies as one has lived. That is one of the great truths which Holy Scripture and the Fathers repeat in many different places. If you live as good Christians, you will be sure to die as good Christians, but if you live badly, you will be sure to die a bad death. The prophet Isaias warns us that the impious man who thinks only of doing evil is in a woeful state, for he will be treated as he deserves. At death he will receive the reward for the work he has done. It is true, however, that sometimes, by a kind of miracle, one may begin badly and finish well, but that happens so rarely that, as St. Jerome puts it, death is generally the echo of life. You think that you will return then to God? No, you will perish in sin. . . .

The Holy Ghost tells us that if we have a friend, we should do him some good before we die. Well, my dear brethren, could one have a better friend than one's soul? Let us do all the good for it that we can, for at the moment when we would like to do our souls good, we shall be able to do no more! . . . Life is short. If you defer changing your ways until the hour of your death, you are blind, for you do not know either the time or the place where you will die, perhaps without any assistance. Who knows if you will not go this night, covered in your sins, before the tribunal of Jesus Christ? . . .

Yes, my dear brethren, as life is, so is death. Do not hope for a miracle, which God but rarely performs. You are living in sin; very well, you will die in sin. . . .

If we desire to die a good death, we must lead a Christian life. And the way for us to prepare for a good death is to model our deaths upon the death of Jesus Christ.

Can the life of the good Christian be anything other than that of a man nailed to the Cross with Jesus Christ?

ε◆ *IF MAN KNEW HIS RELIGION*

NEITHER WEALTH, NOR HONORS, NOR VANITY CAN make a man happy during his life on earth, but only attachment to the service of God, when we are fortune enough to realize that and to carry it out properly. The woman who is held in contempt by her husband is not unhappy in her state because she is held in contempt but because she does not know her religion or because she does not practice what her religion tells her she should do. Teach her her religion, and from the moment that you see her practice it, she will cease to complain and to consider herself unhappy. Oh! How happy man would be, even on this earth, if he knew his religion! . . .

What power that person who is near to God possesses when he loves Him and serves Him faithfully! Alas, my dear brethren, anyone who is despised by worldly people, who appears to be unimportant and humble, look at him when he masters the very will and power of God Himself. Look at a Moses, who compels the Lord to grant pardon to three hundred thousand men who were indeed guilty. Look at Josue, who commanded the sun to stand still and the sun became immobile, a thing which never happened before and which perhaps will never happen again. Look at the Apostles: simply because they loved God, the devils fled before them, the lame walked, the blind saw, the dead arose to life. Look at St. Benedict, who commanded the rocks to stop in their course and they remained hanging in midair. Look at him who multiplied bread, who made water come out of rocks, and who disposed of the stones and the forest as easily as if they were wisps of straw. Look at a St. Francis of Paula who commands the fish to come to hear the word of God and they respond to his call with such loyalty that they applaud his words. Look at a St. John who commands the birds to keep silent and they obey him. Look at many others who walk the seas without any human aid. Very well! Now take a look at all those impious people and all those famous ones of the world with all their wit and all their knowledge for achieving everything. Alas! Of what are they really capable? Nothing at all. And why not? Unless it is because they are not attached to the service of God. But how powerful and how happy at the same time is the person who knows his religion and who practices what it commands.

Alas, my dear brethren, the man who lives according to the direction of his passions and abandons the service of God is both unhappy and capable of so little! Put an army of one hundred thousand men around a dead man and let them employ all their power to bring him back to life. No, no, my dear children, he will not come to life again. But let someone who is despised by the world, but who enjoys the friendship of God, command this dead man to take up life again; immediately you will see him arise and walk. We have other proofs of this, too. If it were necessary to be wealthy or to be very learned to serve God, a great many people would be unable to do it. But, no, my dear children, extensive learning or great wealth are not at all necessary for the service of God. On the contrary, they are often a very big obstacle to it. Yes, my dear brethren, let us be rich or poor, in whatever state we may be, learned or otherwise, we can please God and save our souls. . . .

Listen to me for one moment and you will see that only the service of God will console us and make us happy in the midst of all the miseries of life. To accomplish it, you do not need to leave either your belongings, or your parents, or even your friends, unless they are leading you to sin. You have no need to go and spend the rest of your lives in the desert to weep there for your sins. If that were necessary for us, indeed, we should be very happy to have such a remedy for our ills. But no, a father and a mother of a family can serve God by living with their children and bringing them up in a Christian way. A servant can very easily serve God and his master, with nothing to stop him.

No, my dear brethren, the way of life which means serving God changes nothing in all that we have to do. On the contrary, we simply do better all the things we must do.

ཙ་ *THOUGHTS ON THE WAY TO CHURCH*

WHEN OUR DUTY CALLS US TO A HOLY PLACE, might not anyone say that we resemble criminals being led before their judges to be condemned to the worst possible tortures, rather than Christians whom love alone should lead to God? How very blind we are, my dear brethren, to have so little heart for the things of Heaven, while at the same time we are so taken up with the things of the world!

Indeed, when it is a question of temporal matters or even of pleasures, everyone will be preoccupied with them. They will think about them in advance. They will meditate upon them. But, unfortunately, when the question is one of the service of our God and the salvation of our poor souls the whole thing becomes a matter of routine and inconceivable indifference. Suppose someone wants to speak to a very important or influential person and to ask him some favor. He will dwell upon the matter for a long time in advance. He will consult others whom he thinks better educated or more experienced than himself in order to find out in what way he should approach this person. He will appear before him with that modest and respectful bearing which, generally speaking, the presence of such a personage inspires. But when he comes into the house of God, ah, there is no more of that sort of thing. No one thinks then of what he is about to do or of what he is about to ask of God.

Tell me, my dear brethren, who is there who, as he is going along to the church, is saying to himself: Where am I going? Is it to the house of a man or to the palace of a king? Oh, no, it is into the house of my God, into the dwelling place of Him Who loves me more than Himself, since He died for me, Whose compassionate eyes are aware of my actions, Whose ears are attentive to my prayers, always ready to hear my prayers and to forgive. Filled with these blessed thoughts, why would we not exclaim with the holy King David: "O my soul, rejoice that you are about to enter the house of the Lord," to give Him your homage, to show Him your needs, to listen to His divine words, to ask Him for His graces.

Oh what things I have to say to Him, what graces I have to ask of Him, what gratitude I have to pay Him! I will speak to Him of all my worries, and I know that He will console me. I will admit my faults to Him, and He will forgive me. I am going to talk to Him of my family, and He will bless it with all sorts of mercies. Yes, my God, I shall adore You in Your holy temple, and I shall return from there filled with all sorts of benedictions.

Tell me, my dear brethren, is that the sort of thought which occupies you when your religious duties call you to church? Are those indeed the thoughts you have, after having wasted the entire morning in discussing your sales and your purchases, or at the least, some other entirely useless matters? You come along in a hurry to hear a Mass which often is half-finished. Alas! If I dare to put into words how many go to visit the god of drunkenness before their Creator; and, coming to church full of wine, they will talk and concern themselves with temporal matters right up to the very door! Oh! Dear God! Are these Christians, who ought to be living like angels upon earth?

What of you, my good woman, are your thoughts any better now that you have occupied your mind and part of your time in thinking how you were going to dress, so that you might please the people you know; and then you come to a place where you should come only to lament for your sins? Indeed, too often the priest is ascending the altar while you are still turning around and around, looking at yourself in front of a mirror. Ah, dear God! Are these really Christians who have taken You for their Model, You, Whose whole life was spent amidst scorn and tears? Listen, my dear young lady, to what St. Ambrose, the Bishop of Milan, has to teach you. As he was in the doorway of the church one day and saw a young person approaching dressed with the greatest of care, he spoke to her. "Where are you going, young woman?" he asked. She told him that she was going to church. "You are going to the church," the holy Bishop said to her, "but one might rather think that you are going to the dance or to a play or a spectacle. Go away, sinful woman, and weep for your sins in secret, and do not come to the church to insult with your frivolous adornments a crucified God."

Dear Lord! How our century has provided us with. . . .[13] How many people when they are coming to the church think of nothing else except themselves and their clothes and styles. They enter the temple of the Lord saying from the depths of their hearts: "Have a good look at me." When we see such wrong dispositions, how can we help but shed tears?

And you, fathers and mothers, what are your dispositions when you come to church, to the Mass? Alas! We must admit it with sorrow that most frequently the fathers and mothers that we see are coming into the church when the priest is already on the altar, or even in the pulpit!

Ah, you will tell me, we came as soon as we could. We have other things to do.

Undoubtedly you have other things to do. But I know very well, too, that if you did not leave until Sunday the one hundred and one things in your homes which you should have done on Saturday, and if you had got up a little earlier in the morning, you would have done them all before holy Mass, and you would have arrived at the church before the priest had ascended the altar. It can be the same thing, too, with your children and your servants: if you had not been giving them orders until the very

[13] Sentence incomplete.—Trans.

last stroke of the Mass bell, they would have arrived at the church at the beginning. I do not know whether God will receive all these excuses easily; I hardly think so.

But why, my dear brethren, should I speak of particular cases? Surely it is the majority of you who behave in this way. Yes, when you are called to church so that the graces of God may be administered to you, anyone may see this lack of enthusiasm in you, this indifference, this boredom which consumes you, this practically general inattention. Tell me, where will you see the majority of the general congregation when the services are beginning? Are the Vespers not half said by the time you arrive?

We have work to do, you tell me.

Well, my friends, if you were to tell me that you have neither faith, nor love of God, nor the desire to save your poor souls, I would believe you much better. Alas! What can anyone think of all that? . . . There is a great deal to lament in what is to be seen of the dispositions of the majority of Christians! A great many seem to come to church only in spite of themselves or, if I dare to put it that way, as if someone were dragging them there. From the house to the church, temporal matters only are discussed. A group of young girls together will talk about nothing except style, beauty, and all the rest of it; the young men only of games and amusements or of other matters which are more evil. The fathers or the masters of households will chat about their property or business, about buying and selling. The mothers are preoccupied only with their households and their children. No one will go so far as to deny that. Alas! Not a single thought will be given to the happiness they are about to have, not a single reflection on the needs of their poor souls or those of their children or their servants! They enter the holy temple without respect, without attention, and a great many of them as late as is possible. How many others do not even go to the trouble of coming in at all, but stay outside, in order to find better ways of distracting themselves? The word of God does not trouble their consciences: they look around at those who are coming and going. . . . Dear God! Are these really the Christians for whom You suffered so much in order to make them happy? And this is all they think of it? . . .

With dispositions like that, how many sins must be committed during the services? How many people must commit more sins on Sunday than during all the rest of the week! . . . Listen to what St. Martin has to tell us. . . . While he was singing the Mass with St. Brice, his disciple, he noticed the latter smiling. After it was all over, he asked him what had made him smile. St. Brice replied: "Father, I saw something extraordinary while we were singing the holy Mass. Behind the altar I saw a devil and he was writing on a huge sheet of parchment the sins which were being committed in the church, and his sheet was rather full before the Mass was finished. So the devil took the sheet of parchment between his teeth and tugged it so hard that he tore it into shreds. That was what made me smile."

What sins, and even mortal sins, we commit during the services by our lack of devotion and recollection! Alas! What has become of those happy times when Christians passed not only the day but even the greater part of the nights in the church, mourning for their sins and singing the praises of God? See, even in the Old Testament, see holy Anna the prophetess, who withdrew into a tribune in order to leave the service of God no more. Look at the holy old man Simeon. See again Zachary and so many others who passed the greater portion of their lives in the service of the Lord. And note, too, how marvelous and how precious were the graces which God bestowed upon them. To reward Anna, God willed that she should be the very first to recognize our Lord. The holy old man Simeon was also the first, after St. Joseph, to have the happiness, the very great happiness, of holding the Savior of the world in his arms. The holy Zachary was chosen to be the father of a child destined to be the ambassador of the Eternal Father in announcing the coming of His Son into the world. What wonderful graces does God not grant to those who make it their duty to come to visit Him in His holy temple as much as they possibly can. . . .

❧ *YOU ARE SURPRISED, BUT NOT I!*

WHY IS IT, THEN, YOU ARE GOING TO ASK ME, THAT we assist at so many Masses and yet we are always the same? Alas, my dear brethren, it is because we are there in body but not in spirit and that rather our coming there completes our condemnation because of the bad dispositions with which we assist. Alas! For all those badly heard Masses which, far from insuring our salvation, harden us the more. When our Lord appeared to St. Mechtilde, He said to her: "Know this, my child, that the saints will assist at the death of all those who have heard Mass devoutly, to help them to die well, to defend them against the temptations of the Devil, and to offer their souls to My Father." What wonderful happiness for us, my dear brethren, to be helped at this formidable moment by as many saints as we have heard Masses! . . .

No, my dear children, we need never fear that the Mass hinders us in the fulfillment of our temporal affairs; it is altogether the other way around. We may be sure that all will go better and that even our business will succeed better than if we have the misfortune not to assist at Mass. Here is a splendid example of that. It concerns two artisans who belonged to the same trade and who lived in the same little town. One of them, who had a very large family and never missed hearing Mass every day, lived very comfortably by his trade, but the other, on the contrary, who had no family, worked all day and part of the night, and very often on the holy day of Sunday, and still had the greatest difficulty in the world in making ends meet. The latter, when he saw how well things were going for the other man, asked him one day when he met him how he managed to make enough to maintain so comfortably a family as large as his. As for himself, he said, although there were only his wife and himself and he never stopped working, he was often short of everything. The other replied that if he so wished, he would show him the following day where he made his profit. Delighted with this good news, the unsuccessful artisan could hardly wait until the following day so that he might learn how to make his fortune. True to his word, his friend called for him. So there he was, setting off in great heart and, full of confidence, following his friend who brought him to church, where they heard Mass. When they came out the friend said, quite at his ease, "You can go back to your work now." The same thing took place the following day, but on the third day, when the friend came to bring the unsuccessful artisan along to Mass, the latter objected. "What is all this about?" he asked. "If I want to go to Mass, I know the way without your taking the trouble to come and get me. That is not what I wanted to know, but the place where you find all the money that enables you to live so comfortably. I wanted to see whether, if I did the same as you, I could get something out of it, too."

"My good friend," said the other to him, "I do not know any other place than the church, and no other method than that of hearing Mass every day of the week. I assure you that I have never used any other means to acquire the money which surprises you. But have you yourself not seen where Jesus Christ tells us in the Gospel to seek first the kingdom of God and that all the rest will be added unto us?"

Are you surprised at this story, my dear brethren? I am not. It is only what we see every day of our lives in those homes where there is some religion. Those who come often to holy Mass manage their affairs much better than those whose weak faith makes them think that they have no time for Mass. Alas, if only we put all our trust in God and relied on our own efforts for nothing, how much happier we should be than we are!

Yes, you will tell me, but if we have nothing, no one is going to give us anything.

What do you want God to give you when—as is shown by the fact that you do not give even the time to saying your morning and night prayers and that you are quite content to come to Mass once a week—you depend solely on your own efforts and not at all on Him? You have no knowledge of the resources of the providence of God for anyone who confides and trusts in Him. Do you want a more striking proof of this? It is before your eyes. Look at your pastor and examine his case in the light of God's providence.

Oh, you say, that is because people give to you.

But who gives to me, unless it is the providence of God? That is the source of my treasures and nothing else. Alas, that man should be blind enough to worry and fret so much as to damn himself and yet be quite unhappy in this world. If you have the great happiness to think a lot about your salvation and to assist at holy Mass as much as you can, you will soon see the proof of what I am telling you.

✒ WHEN YOU GO BACK HOME . . .

ON HER RETURN TO HER KINGDOM, THE QUEEN OF Sheba could never weary of relating all that she had seen in the temple of Solomon; she talked of it unceasingly, with fresh pleasure. The same thing should happen to the Christian who has assisted properly at holy Mass. When he comes back to his house, he ought to have a talk with his children and his servants and ask them what they have retained of it and what touched them most. Alas! Dear God, what am I going to say? . . . How many fathers and mothers, masters and mistresses are there who, if someone wanted to talk to them about what they had heard at Mass, would laugh at all that and say that they were tired of it, that they knew enough about it. . . . Although generally speaking it seems that people still listen to the holy word of God, the moment they come out of church, they fall into all sorts of careless and frivolous ways. They get up with a sudden rush. They hurry. They jostle at the door. Often the priest has not even come down from the altar when they are already outside the door, and there they give themselves up to discussions upon all sorts of secular subjects.

Do you know what the result of this kind of thing is, my dear brethren? This is it. People derive no profit and gain no benefit from what they have heard and seen in the house of God. What graces have been lost! What means of salvation trodden underfoot! What a misfortune that is, to turn to our loss what should have helped so much to save us! You can see for yourselves how many of these services are a burden to the majority of Christians! For those few moments, they stay in the church as if it were some kind of prison, and as soon as they are out, you will hear them shouting at the door, like prisoners who have been given liberty. Are we not quite frequently obliged to close the door of the church in order not to be deafened by their continual noise?

Dear God, are these really Christians, who ought to leave Your holy temple with minds filled only with all kinds of good thoughts and desires? Should not they be seeking to engrave these in their memory, that they may never lose them and that they may put them into practice as soon as the opportunity presents itself? Alas! The number of those who assist at the services with attention and who try to profit from them is a little like the number of the elect: ah, how small it is!

੨ CLEAR YOUR MINDS

IF YOU DESIRE THE WORSHIP THAT YOU GIVE TO GOD to be pleasing to Him and valuable for the salvation of your soul, put it properly into practice. Begin by preparing for holy

Mass as soon as you are awake, uniting yourself to all the Masses which are being said at that moment. When the bell rings to call you to the house of God, consider the fact that it is Jesus Christ Himself calling you. Start out immediately, so that you will have a moment to meditate upon the tremendous act at which you are about to assist. Do not say, like those people who have no religion, that you have plenty of time, that you will be there soon enough. But say, rather, with the Holy Prophet: "I rejoice when I am told that we are going into the house of the Lord."

When you come out from your home, think about what you are going to do and what you are going to ask of God. Begin by clearing your mind of earthly matters so that you will be thinking of God only. Avoid all sorts of unnecessary conversations which serve no other purpose than to make you hear Mass badly. When you enter the church, recall to yourself what the holy patriarch Jacob said: How awesome is this place! How holy it is! It is truly the house of God and the gateway to heaven!

When you get to your place, humble yourself profoundly as you think of your own unworthiness and the greatness of your God, Who, nevertheless, in spite of your sins, wishes to suffer you in His holy presence. Make an act of faith with all your heart. Ask God to give you the grace to lose none of the many favors which He grants to those who come here with good dispositions. Open your heart so that the word of God may enter it, take root in it, and bear fruit there for eternal life. Before leaving the church, do not fail to thank God for the graces He has just given you and go straight home, fully occupied with the thoughts of what you have seen and heard.

Yes, my dear children, if we conducted ourselves in this manner, we should never come away from the services of the Church without being filled with a fresh desire for heaven and a new disgust for ourselves and the things of this earth. Our hearts and our minds would be given over altogether to God and not at all

to the world. Then the house of God would truly be for us the
gateway to Heaven. That is what I desire for you.

੭੶ *WE ARE KEEPING A FEAST*

IN THE EARLY DAYS OF THE CHURCH, THE FAITHFUL
of one province, or district, used to come together publicly on
the feast day of a saint in order to have the happiness of participating in all the graces which God bestows on such days.
The office of the vigil was started. The evening and night were
spent in prayer at the tomb of the saint. The faithful heard the
word of God. They sang hymns and canticles in honor of the
saint. After passing the night so devoutly, they heard Mass, at
which all those assisting had the happiness of going to Holy
Communion. Then they all withdrew, praising God for the tri-
umphs He had accorded the saint and the graces He had bestowed in response to the latter's intercession. After that, my
dear brethren, who could doubt but that God pours out His
graces with abundance upon such a reunion of the faithful and
that the saints themselves are happy to be the patrons of such
people. That was the way in which the feast days of patron
saints were celebrated in olden times.

What do you think of that? Is it thus that we celebrate such
feasts today? Alas! If the first Christians were to come back
upon this earth, would they not tell us that our feasts are no
different from those that the pagans kept? Is it not the general
rule that God is most seriously offended on these holy days?
Does it not seem, rather, that we combine our money and our
energies together to multiply sin almost to infinity?

What are we concerned with on the vigil of such feasts, and
even for several days beforehand? Is it not with spending foolish and unnecessary money? And all this time poor people are
dying of hunger and our sins are calling down upon us the anger
of God to the point where eternity would not be sufficient to

satisfy for them. You should pass the night in repentance and remorse, in considering how very little you have followed the example of your patron saint. And yet you consecrate that time to preparing everything that will flatter your gluttony! Might it not be said that this day is one for pure self-indulgence and debauchery? Do parents and friends come, as in former times, to enjoy the happiness of participating in the graces which God bestows at the intercession of a patron saint? They come, but only to pass this feast day almost wholly at the table. In former times, the religious services were much longer than they are to-day, and still they seemed always too short. Nowadays you will see even fathers of families who, during the performance of the offices, are at table filling themselves with food and wine. The first Christians invited each other in order to multiply their good works and their prayers. Today it seems rather as if people invite each other so that they can multiply the sins and the orgies and the excesses in which they indulge in eating and drinking. Does anyone think God will not demand an account of even a penny wrongly spent? Does it not seem that we celebrate the feast only to insult our holy Patron and to increase our ingratitude?

Let us look a little closer, my dear brethren, and we shall realize that we are far from imitating Him whom God has given us for a model. He passed His life in penance and in sorrow. He died in torments. What is more, I am sure that there are parishes where more sins are committed on those days than during all the rest of the year. The Lord told the Jews that their feasts were an abomination and that He would take the filth of their feasts and throw it in their faces. He wished to make us understand by this how greatly He is offended on those days which should be passed in weeping for our sins and in prayer.

We read in the Gospel that Jesus Christ came on earth to enlighten souls with the fire of divine love. But we can believe that the Devil also roams around on earth to light an impure fire in the hearts of Christians and that what he promotes with the greatest frenzy are balls and dances. I have debated for a long time whether I should speak to you about a matter so difficult to get you to understand and so little thought upon by the Christians of our days, who are blinded by their passions. If your faith were not so weak that it might be extinguished in your hearts in the blink of an eye, you would understand the enormity of the abyss towards which you precipitate yourselves in giving yourselves over with such abandon to these wretched amusements. But you will tell me. For you to talk to us about dances and about the evil that takes place at them is just a waste of time. We will indulge neither more nor less in them. I firmly believe that, since Tertullian assures us that very many refused to become Christians rather than deprive themselves of such pleasures.

BE RELIGIOUS OR BE DAMNED!

THERE IS ALWAYS THE PERSON WHO SAYS TO ME: "What harm can there be in enjoying oneself for a while? I do no wrong to anyone; I do not want to be religious or to become a religious! If I do not go to dances, I will be living in the world like someone dead!"

My good friend, you are wrong. Either you will be religious or you will be damned. What is a religious person? This is nothing other than a person who fulfills his duties as a Christian. You say that I shall achieve nothing by talking to you about dances and that you will indulge neither more nor less in them. You are wrong again. In ignoring or despising the instructions of your pastor, you draw down upon yourself fresh chastisements from God, and I, on my side, will achieve quite a lot by fulfilling my duties. At the hour of my death, God will ask me not if you have fulfilled your duties but if I have taught you what you must do in order to fulfill them. You say, too, that I shall never break down your resistance to the point of making you believe that there is harm in amusing yourself for a little while in dancing? You do not wish to believe that there is any harm in it? Well, that is your affair. As far as I am concerned, it is sufficient for me to tell you in such a way as will insure that you do understand, even if you want to do it all the same. By doing this I am doing all that I should do. That should not irritate you: your pastor is doing his duty. But, you will say, the Commandments of God do not forbid dancing, nor does Holy Scripture, either. Perhaps you have not examined them very closely. Follow me for a moment and you will see that there is not a Commandment of God which dancing does not cause to be transgressed, nor a Sacrament which it does not cause to be profaned.

You know as well as I do that these kinds of follies and wild extravagances are not ordinarily indulged in, but on Sundays and feast days. What, then, will a young girl or a boy do who have decided to go to the dance? What love will they have for God? Their minds will be wholly occupied with their preparations to attract the people with whom they hope to be mixing. Let us suppose that they say their prayers—how will they say them? Alas, only God knows that! Besides, what love for God can be felt by anyone who is thinking and breathing nothing but the love of pleasures and of creatures? You will admit that it is impossible to please God and the world. That can never be.

God forbids swearing. Alas! What quarrels, what swearing, what blasphemies are uttered as a result of the jealousy that arises between these young people when they are at such gatherings! Have you not often had disputes or fights there? Who could count the crimes that are committed at these diabolical gatherings? The Third Commandment commands us to sanctify the holy day of Sunday. Can anyone really believe that a boy who has passed several hours with a girl, whose heart is like a furnace, is really thus satisfying this precept? St. Augustine has good reason to say that men would be better to work their land and girls to carry on with their spinning than to go dancing; the evil would be less. The Fourth Commandment of God commands children to honor their parents. These young people who frequent the dances, do they have the respect and the submission to their parents' wishes which they should have? No, they certainly do not; they cause them the utmost worry and distress between the way they disregard their parents' wishes and the way they put their money to bad use, while sometimes even taunting them with their old-fashioned outlook and ways. What sorrow should not such parents feel, that is, if their faith is not yet extinct, at seeing their children given over to such pleasures or, to speak more plainly, to such licentious ways? These children are no longer Heaven-bent, but are fattening for Hell. Let us suppose that the parents have not yet lost the Faith. . . . Alas! I dare not go any further! . . . What blind parents! . . . What lost children! . . .

Is there any place, any time, any occasion wherein so many sins of impurity are committed as the dancehalls and their sequels? Is it not in these gatherings that people are most violently prompted against the holy virtue of purity? Where else but there are the senses so strongly urged towards pleasurable excitement? If we go a little more closely into this, should we not almost die of horror at the sight of so many crimes which are committed? Is it not at these gatherings that the Devil so furiously kindles the fire of impurity in the hearts of the young people in order to annihilate in them the grace of Baptism? Is it not there that Hell enslaves as many souls as it wishes? If, in spite of the absence of occasions and the aids of prayer, a Christian has so much difficulty in preserving purity of heart, how could he possibly preserve that virtue in the midst of so many sources which are capable of breaking it down?

"Look," says St. John Chrysostom, "at this worldly and flighty young woman, or rather at this flaming brand of diabolical fire who by her beauty and her flamboyant attire lights in the heart of that young man the fire of concupiscence. Do you not see them, one as much as the other, seeking to charm one another by their airs and graces and all sorts of tricks and wiles? Count up, unfortunate sinner, if you can, the number of your bad thoughts, of your evil desires and your sinful actions. Is it not there that you heard those airs that please the ears, that inflame and burn hearts and make of these assemblies furnaces of shamelessness?"

Is it not there, my dear brethren, that the boys and the girls drink at the fountain of crime, which very soon, like a torrent or a river bursting its banks, will inundate, ruin, and poison all its surroundings? Go on, shameless fathers and mothers, go on into Hell, where the fury of God awaits you, you and all the good actions you have done in letting your children run such risks. Go on, they will not be long in joining you, for you have outlined the road plainly for them. Go and count the number of years that your boys and girls have lost, go before your Judge to give an account of your lives, and you will see that your pastor had reason to forbid these kinds of diabolical pleasures! . . .

Ah, you say, you are making more of it than there really is!

I say too much about it? Very well, then. Listen. Did the Holy Fathers of the Church say too much about it? St. Ephraim tells us that dancing is the perdition of girls and women, the blinding of men, the grief of angels, and the joy of the devils. Dear God, can anyone really have their eyes bewitched to such an extent that they will still want to believe that there is no harm in it, while all the time it is the rope by which the Devil pulls the most souls into Hell? . . . Go on, poor parents, blind and lost, go on and scorn what your pastor is telling you! Go on! Continue the way you are going! Listen to everything and profit nothing by it! There is no harm in it? Tell me, then, what did you renounce on the day of your Baptism? Or on what conditions was Baptism given to you? Was it not on the condition of your taking a vow in the face of Heaven and earth, in the presence of Jesus Christ upon the altar, that you would renounce Satan and all his works and pomps, for the whole of your lives—or in other words that you would renounce sin and the pleasures and vanities of the world?

Was it not because you promised that you would be willing to follow in the steps of a crucified God? Well then, is this not truly to violate those promises made at your Baptism and to profane this Sacrament of mercy? Do you not also profane the Sacrament of Confirmation, in exchanging the Cross of Jesus Christ, which you have received, for vain and showy dress, in being ashamed of that Cross, which should be your glory and your happiness?

St. Augustine tells us that those who go to dances truly renounce Jesus Christ in order to give themselves to the Devil. What a horrible thing that is! To drive out Jesus Christ after having received Him in your hearts! "Today," says St. Ephraim, "they unite themselves to Jesus Christ and tomorrow to the Devil." Alas! What a Judas is that person who, after receiving our Lord, goes then to sell Him to Satan in these gatherings, where he will be reuniting himself with everything that is most vicious! And when it comes to the Sacrament of Penance, what a contradiction is such a life! A Christian, who after one single sin should spend the rest of his life in repentance, thinks only of giving himself up to all these worldly pleasures! A great many profane the Sacrament of Extreme Unction by making indecent movements with the feet, the hands and the whole body, which one day must be sanctified by the holy oils. Is not the Sacrament of Holy Order insulted by the contempt with which the instructions of the pastor are considered? But when we come to the Sacrament of Matrimony, alas! What infidelities are not contemplated in these assemblies? It seems then that everything is admissible. How blind must anyone be who thinks there is no harm in it! . . .

The Council of Aix-la-Chapelle forbids dancing, even at weddings. And St. Charles Borromeo, the Archbishop of Milan, says that three years of penance were given to someone who had danced and that if he went back to it, he was threatened with excommunication. If there were no harm in it, then were the Holy Fathers and the Church mistaken? But who tells you that there is no harm in it? It can only be a libertine, or a flighty and worldly girl, who are trying to smother their remorse of conscience as best they can. Well, there are priests, you say, who do not speak about it in Confession or who, without permitting it, do not refuse absolution for it. Ah! I do not know whether there are priests who are so blind, but I am sure that those who go looking for easygoing priests are going looking for a passport which will lead them to Hell. For my own part, if I went dancing, I should not want to receive absolution not having a real determination not to go back dancing.

Listen to St. Augustine and you will see if dancing is a good action. He tells us that "dancing is the ruin of souls, a reversal of all decency, a shameful spectacle, a public profession of crime." St. Ephraim calls it "the ruin of good morals and the nourishment of vice." St. John Chrysostom: "A school of public unchastity." Tertullian: "The temple of Venus, the consistory of shamelessness, and the citadel of all the depravities." "Here is a girl who dances," says St. Ambrose, "but she is the daughter of an adulteress because a Christian woman would teach her daughter modesty, a proper sense of shame, and not dancing!"

Alas! How many young people are there who since they have been going to dances do not frequent the Sacraments, or do so only to profane them! How many poor souls there are who have lost therein their religion and their faith! How many will never open their eyes to their unhappy state except when they are falling into Hell! . . .

ॐ *YOUR PRAYERS ARE ONLY AN INSULT*

THERE ARE SOME WHO DERIVE SATISFACTION FROM the virtues they practice because their tendencies are all that way. For example, a mother will pride herself on the fact that she gives some alms, that she frequents the Sacraments, that she even reads some spiritual books—yet she sees without dismay that her children are keeping away from the Sacraments. Her children do not make their Easter duty, yet this mother, from time to time, gives them permission to go to amusements, to dances, to weddings, and sometimes to the winter gatherings.[14] She loves to see her daughters appearing in public; she thinks that if they do not frequent these places of debauchery, no one will know them and they will not be able to find themselves husbands and homes. Yes, undoubtedly they would be unknown—but only to the libertines. Yes, my dear brethren, they will not find themselves husbands from among those who would treat them like the most wretched slaves. This mother loves to see them well turned out; this mother loves to see them in the company of some young men who are wealthier than they are. After certain prayers and some good works, which certainly she will do, she thinks herself to be on the road to Heaven.

Carry on, my good mother; you are only a blind hypocrite; you have only the appearance of virtue. You set your mind at rest with the thought that you make some visits to the Blessed Sacrament; without any doubt that is a good thing; but your daughter is at a dance; but your daughter is at the cabaret with libertines, and they will be spewing out nothing but one kind or another of indecency; but your daughter, tonight, is in a place where she should not be. Go away, blind and abandoned mother, go out and leave your prayers. Do you not see that you are doing as the Jews did, who bent the knee before Jesus Christ to make a semblance of adoring Him? So, then, you come to adore God, while your children are out to crucify Him. Poor blind creature, you do not know either what you say or what you do. Your prayers are only an insult which you offer to God. Begin by going to find your daughter, who is losing

14 See Footnote 2.

her soul; then you may return to God to ask Him for your conversion.

A father thinks that it is quite enough to maintain good order in his house; he will not have anyone swearing or using obscene words. That is very good. But he has no scruple about allowing his boys to go to amusements, to fairs, and all sorts of pleasures like that. This same father permits work to be done on Sundays on the slightest pretext, even such as not to go against the wishes of his reapers or his threshers. However, you see him in church adoring God, even prostrate before Him: he is trying to avoid the slightest distraction. But tell me, my friends, how do you suppose God can look upon such people as that? Carry on, my poor friend, you are blind. Go and learn your duties and then you may come to offer your prayers to God. Do you not see that you are doing the work of Pontius Pilate, who recognized Jesus Christ and who yet condemned Him?

You will see this other man, who is charitable, who gives alms, who is touched by the poverty of his neighbor. That is quite good. But he allows his children to live in the greatest ignorance. Perhaps they do not even know what they should do in order to be saved. Go along, my poor man. You are blind. Your alms and your sympathy are leading you, with great steps, straight to Hell. Here is another who has plenty of good qualities. He likes to help everyone. But he cannot tolerate his unfortunate wife or his poor children, upon whom he heaps insults, and possibly even ill-treats. Carry on, my friend, your religion is worth nothing.

This one thinks that he is quite good because he is not a blasphemer or a thief, or even unchaste, but he goes to no trouble at all to correct those thoughts of hatred, of revenge, of envy, and of jealousy which fill his soul almost every day. My friend, your religion can only ruin you.

We see others, too, who are all full of pious practices, who become full of scruples at omitting some prayers they usually say. They would think themselves lost if they were not at Holy

Communion on certain days when they have the habit of receiving, but trifles make them impatient and grumblers. A mere word which they did not care for will fill them with coldness and dislike. They will have difficulty in being civil to their neighbor; they will want to have nothing to do with him; on different pretexts, they will avoid his company; they will find that someone has been behaving badly in respect of them.

Go away, you poor hypocrites, go and become converted; after that you may have recourse to the Sacraments, which, in your state, without knowing it, you are only profaning with your wrongly understood devotion.

৯ৡ *PURITY IS NOT KNOWN*

ALAS, MY DEAR BRETHREN, HOW LITTLE PURITY IS known in the world; how little we value it; what little care we take to preserve it; what little zeal we have in asking God for it, since we cannot have it of ourselves.

No, my dear brethren, it is not known to those notorious and seasoned libertines who wallow in and trail through the slime of their depravities, whose hearts are . . . roasted and burned by an impure fire . . .[15] Alas, very far from seeking to extinguish it, they do not cease to inflame it and to stir it up by their glances, their desires, and their actions. What state will such a soul be in when it appears before its God!

Purity! No, my dear brethren, this beautiful virtue is not known by such a person whose lips are but an opening and a supply pipe which Hell uses to vomit its impurities upon the earth and who subsists upon these as upon his daily bread. Alas! That poor soul is only an object of horror in Heaven and on earth!

No, my dear brethren, this gracious virtue of purity is not known to those young men whose eyes and hands are defiled by

[15] Sentence incomplete.—Trans.

glances and . . .[16] Oh God, how many souls does this sin drag down to Hell! . . . No, my dear brethren, this beautiful virtue is not known to those worldly and corrupt girls who make so many preparations and take so many cares to draw the eyes of the world towards themselves, who by their affected and indecent dress announce publicly that they are evil instruments which Hell makes use of to ruin souls—those souls which cost so much in labors and tears and torments to Jesus Christ! . . . Look at them, these unfortunates, and you will see that a thousand devils surround their heads and their breasts. Oh, my God, how can the earth support such servants of Hell? An even more astounding thing to understand is how their mothers endure them in a state unworthy of a Christian! If I were not afraid of going too far, I would tell those mothers that they are worth no more than their daughters.

Alas! This sinful heart and those impure eyes are but sources of poison which bring death to anyone who looks at or listens to them. How do such monsters of iniquity dare to present themselves before a God Who is so holy and so set against impurity! Alas! Their poor lives are nothing but an accumulation of fuel which they amass to increase the flames of Hell through all eternity.

But, my dear brethren, let us leave a subject which is so disgusting and so revolting to a Christian, whose purity should imitate that of Jesus Christ Himself, and let us return to our beautiful virtue, which raises us to Heaven, which opens to us the adorable Heart of our Lord and draws down upon us all sorts of spiritual and temporal blessings. . . .

St. James tells us that this virtue comes from Heaven and that we shall never have it unless we ask it of God. We should, therefore, frequently ask God to give us purity in our eyes, in our speech, and in all our actions. . . .

Finally, we should have a great devotion to the Blessed Virgin if we wish to preserve this lovely virtue; that is very evi-

[16] Sentence incomplete.—Trans.

dent, since she is the queen, the model, and the patron of virgins. . . .

❧ *THE SERVICE OF THE BLESSED VIRGIN*

IF I WANTED TO, I WOULD SHOW YOU THAT IN ALL walks of life there have been great servants of the Blessed Virgin. I would find for you, among them, those who begged their bread from door to door. I would find for you, among them, those whol lived in much the same sort of state in life as many of you. I would find them for you among the wealthy, and in great number, too. We read in the Gospel that our Lord always treated people with great tenderness, except for one type of people whom He treated with severity; these were the Pharisees, and they were so treated because they were proud and hardened in sin. They would willingly have hindered, if they could, the accomplishment of the will of the Father. What is more, our Lord called them "whited sepulchers, hypocrites, brood of vipers, offspring of vipers, who devour the breasts of their mothers."

We can say the same thing on the subject of devotion to the Blessed Virgin. All Christians have a great devotion to Mary except those old and hardened sinners who, for a very long time, having lost the faith, wallow in the slime of their brute passions. The Devil tries to keep them in this state of blindness until that moment when death opens their eyes. Ah! If they had but the happiness to have recourse to Mary they would not fall into Hell, as will happen to them!

No, my dear children, let us not imitate such people! On the contrary, let us follow the footsteps of all those true servants of Mary. Belonging to this number were St. Charles Borromeo, who always said his rosary on his knees. What is more, he fasted on all vigils of the feasts of the Blessed Virgin. He was so careful about saluting her on the stroke of the bell that when the Angelus rang, wherever he was, he went down on his knees, sometimes even in the middle of the road when it was full of mud. He desired that his whole diocese should have a great devotion to Mary and that her name would be uttered everywhere with the utmost respect. He had a number of chapels built in her honor.

Now then, my dear brethren, why should not we imitate these great saints who obtained so many graces from Mary to preserve them from sin? Have we not the same enemies to fight, the same Heaven to hope for? Yes, Mary always has her eyes upon us. Do we suffer temptations? Let us turn our hearts towards Mary and we shall be delivered.

ৰ OUR INCONSISTENCY

LET US LEAVE, FOR THE MOMENT, THAT EXTERIOR worship which, by a special peculiarity and by an inconsistency full of irreligion, publicly displays your faith and at the same time gives it the lie.

Where is there to be found among you that fraternal charity which, in the principles of your belief, is founded on the most sublime and divine motives? Examine this a little more closely and you will see whether such reproaches are well founded. Your religion is a beautiful one, the Jews and even the pagans tell us, if you do what you are commanded! Not only are you all brothers, but something even more wonderful: all together, you form the same Body of Jesus Christ, whose Flesh and Blood serve you every day as nourishment; you are all members, one of another. It must be admitted that that article of your faith is admirable indeed; it has something divine about it. If you were to act in accordance with your creed, you would be in a position to draw all other peoples to your religion—it is so beautiful, so consoling, and has the promise of such happiness in the life to come. But what makes all the peoples believe that your religion is not what you say it is, is that your conduct is quite the opposite to what your religion commands you.

If anyone were to question your pastors and if it were lawful for them to reveal the secrets of the confessional, they would be able to show that it is the quarrels, the enmities, the spirit of revenge, the jealousies, the scandals, the false rumors and gossip, the lawsuits, and so many other vices which horrify all those peoples whose religion you say is so far removed from yours in holiness. The corruption of morals, which is rife amongst you, keeps back those who are not of your religion from embracing it because if you were really convinced that it is good and divine, you would surely behave in a different way.

ॐ LOVE OF OUR NEIGHBOR

ALL OF OUR RELIGION IS BUT A FALSE RELIGION AND all our virtues are mere illusions and we ourselves are only hypocrites in the sight of God if we have not that universal charity for everyone, for the good and for the bad, for the poor people as well as for the rich, for all those who do us harm as much as for those who do us good.

No, my dear brethren, there is no virtue which will let us know better whether we are the children or God than charity. The obligation we have to love our neighbor is so important that Jesus Christ put it into a Commandment which He placed immediately after that by which He commands us to love Him with all our hearts. He tells us that all the law and the prophets are included in this commandment to love our neighbor. Yes, my dear brethren, we must regard this obligation as the most universal, the most necessary and the most essential to religion and to our salvation. In fulfilling this Commandment, we are fulfilling all others. St. Paul tells us that the other Commandments forbid us to commit adultery, robbery, injuries, false testimonies. If we love our neighbor, we shall not do any of these things because the love we have for our neighbor would not allow us to do him any harm.

⧉ WHO HAS CHARITY?

AH, DEAR LORD, HOW CHRISTIANS ARE DAMNED through lack of charity! No, no, my dear brethren, even if you could perform miracles, you will never be saved if you have not charity. Not to have charity is not to know your religion; it is to have a religion of whim, mood, and inclination. Carry on, carry on, you are only hypocrites and outcasts! Without charity you will never see God, you will never go to Heaven! . . . Give away your wealth, give generous alms to those who love you or who please you, go to Mass every day, go to Holy Communion every day if you wish: you are only hypocrites and outcasts. Continue on your way and you will shortly be in Hell! . . . You cannot endure the faults of your neighbor because he is too tiresome; you do not like his company. Go away, unhappy people, you are but hypocrites, you have only a false religion, which, whatever good you are doing, will lead you to Hell. Oh my God! How rare this virtue is! Alas! It is so rare that they are rare, too, who will be going to Heaven!

I don't want even to see them, you will say. At the church they distract me with all their mannerisms.

Ah, unhappy sinner, say rather that you have no charity and that you are but a miserable creature who loves only those who agree with your sentiments and enter into your interests, who never go against you in anything, who flatter you on the subject of your good works, who love to thank you for your kindnesses, and who give you plenty of attention and recognition. You will do everything for such as these; you do not even mind depriving yourself of some necessity to help them. But if they treated you with contempt or returned your kindness with ingratitude, you would no longer love them. You would never wish to lay eyes upon them. You would avoid their company. You would be very happy to cut short any dealings you have with them. Ah, dear God, what false devotions these are which can only lead us to a place among the outcasts.

If you have any doubt of this, my dear brethren, listen to St. Paul, who will not lead you astray. If, he tells us, I should give my wealth to the poor, if I should work miracles by raising the dead to life, and have not charity, I am nothing other than a hypocrite.

But to convince you even more firmly of it, go over the whole of the Passion of our Lord Jesus Christ. Consult all the lives of the saints; you will find nothing in them which does not conform with this virtue. No, you will not find one of them who did not choose to do good to someone who had done them harm. Look at St. Francis de Sales, who tells us that if he had only one good work to do, he would choose to do it for someone who had done him some wrong rather than for someone who had done him some good service. Alas, my dear brethren, the person who has no charity goes far afield for evil! If someone does him some harm, you see him examining all his actions then. He judges them. He condemns them. He turns them all to evil and is always qute certain that he is right.

But, you will tell me, there are plenty of times when you see people doing wrong and you cannot think otherwise.

My good friend, because you have no charity, you think that they are doing wrong. If you had charity, you would think quite otherwise because you would always think that you could have been mistaken, as so often happens. And to convince you of this, here is an example which I beg of you never to efface from your minds, above all when you think that your neighbor is doing wrong.

It is recounted in the history of the Fathers of the Desert that a hermit named Simeon had remained for many years in solitude when he got the idea of returning to the world. But he asked God that men should never know his intentions during his lifetime. God granted him this grace and he went into the world. He used to pretend to be a fool, and he delivered the possessed from the Devil and he cured the sick. He used to go into the houses of women of evil life and make them swear that they would love him alone, and then he would give them all the money he had. Everyone looked upon him just as a hermit who had become eccentric. They saw him every day, this old man of more than seventy years of age, playing with the children in the streets. At other times he plunged himself into the midst of the public dances, moving around with the crowd while he spoke to them and telling them clearly what wrong they were really doing. But they only looked upon what he said as coming from a fool and simply despised him. At other times he climbed onto the stage and threw stones at all those who were down below. When he saw people who were possessed of the devil, he fell in with them and imitated the possessed as if he also were one of them. He was to be seen hurrying into the inns and mixing with the drunkards. In the markets he rolled around on the ground and did a thousand other things which were very extravagant and extraordinary. Everyone condemned and scorned him. Some looked upon him as a fool. Others thought him a libertine and a bad character who deserved only to be locked up. And yet, my dear children, despite all this, he was actually a saint who sought only scorn to win souls to God, even though everyone judged him to be bad. This shows us that although the very actions of our neighbor appear bad to us, we must not, ourselves, judge them to be bad. Often we judge things to be bad while in the sight of God they are not so. . . .

Yes, my dear children, anyone who has charity does not see the faults of his neighbor. . . .

Whoever possesses charity is sure that Heaven is for him! . . .

That is the happiness which I desire for you.

ᕗ *PRAYING, FASTING, AND PLEASING OURSELVES*

My dear brethren, we read in holy scripture that the Lord, while speaking to His people of the necessity to do good works in order to please Him and to become included in the number of saints, said to them: "The things that I ask are not above your powers; to do them it is not necessary for you to lift yourselves to the clouds nor to cross the seas. All that I command is, so to speak, in your hands, in your hearts, and all around."

I can easily repeat the very same thing to you, my dear brethren. It is true that we shall never have the happiness of going to Heaven unless we do good works, but let us not be afraid of that, my dear children. What Jesus Christ demands of us are not the extraordinary things or those beyond our powers. He does not require that we should be all day in the church or that we should do enormous penances, that is to say, to the extent of ruining our health, or even to that of giving all our substance to the poor (although it is very true that we are obliged to give as much as we possibly can to the poor, which we should do both to please God, Who commands it, and also to atone for our sins). It is also true that we should practice mortification in many things to make reparation for our sins. There is no doubt but that the person who lives without mortifying himself is someone who will never succeed in saving his soul. There is no doubt but that, although we cannot be all day in the church, which yet should be a great joy for us, we do know very well that we should never omit our prayers, at least in the morning and at night.

But, you will say, there are plenty who cannot fast, others who are not able to give alms, and others who have so much to do that often they have great difficulty in saying their prayers in the morning and at night. How can they possibly be saved, then, if it is necessary to pray continuously and to do good works in order to obtain Heaven?

Because all your good works, my dear brethren, amount to prayer, fasting, and almsdeeds, which we can easily perform, as you shall see.

Yes, my dear brethren, even though we may have poor health or even be infirm, there is a fast which we can easily perform. Let us even be quite poor; we can still give alms. And however heavy or demanding our work, we can still pray to Almighty God without interfering with our labors; we can pray night and morning, and even all day long, and here is how we can do it. All the time that we deprive ourselves of anything which it gives us pleasure to do, we are practicing a fast which is very pleasing to God because fasting does not consist solely of privations in eating and drinking, but of denying ourselves that which pleases our taste most. Some mortify themselves in the way they dress; others in the visits they want to make to friends whom they like to see; others in the conversations and discussions which they enjoy. This constitutes a very excellent fast and one which pleases God because it fights self-love and pride and one's reluctance to do things one does not enjoy or to be with people whose characters and ways of behaving are contrary to one's own. You can, without offending God, go into that particular company, but you can deprive yourself of it to please God: there is a type of fasting which is very meritorious. You are in some situation in which you can indulge your appetite? Instead of doing so, you take, without making it obvious, something which appeals to you the least. When you are buying chattels or clothes, you do not choose that which merely appeals to you; there again is a fast whose reward waits for you at the door of Heaven to help you to enter. Yes, my dear brethren, if we want to go about it properly, not only can we find opportunities of practicing fasting every day, but at every moment of the day.

Tell me, now, is there any fasting which would be more pleasing to God than to do and to endure with patience certain things which often are very disagreeable to you? Without mentioning illness, infirmities, or so many other afflictions which are inseparable from our wretched life, how often do we not have the opportunity to mortify ourselves in putting up with what annoys and revolts us? Sometimes it is work which wearies us greatly; sometimes it is some person who annoys us. At another time it may be some humiliation which is very difficult to endure. Well, then, my children, if we put up with all that for God and solely to please Him, these are the fasts which are most agreeable to God and most meritorious in His eyes. You are compelled to work all the year round at very heavy and exacting labor which often seems as if it is going to kill you and which does not give you even the time to draw your breath. Oh, my dear children, what treasures would you be storing up for Heaven, if you so desired, by doing just what you do and in the midst of your labors having the wisdom and the foresight to lift up your hearts to God and say to Him: "My good Jesus, I unite my labors to Your labors, my sufferings to Your sufferings; give me the grace to be always content in the state in which You have placed me! I will bless Your holy Name in all that happens to me!" Yes, my dear children, if you had the great happiness to behave in this way, all your trials, all your labors, would become like most precious fruits which you would offer to God at the hour of your death. That, my children, is how everyone is his own state in life can practice a kind of fasting which is very meritorious and which will be of the greatest value to him for eternal life.

I have been telling you, too, that there is a certain type of almsgiving which everyone can perform. You see quite well that almsgiving does not consist solely in feeding those who are hungry and giving clothes to those who have none. It consists in all the services which one renders to a neighbor, whether of body or soul, when they are done in a spirit of charity. When we have only a little, very well, let us give a little; and when we have nothing, let us lend if we can. If you cannot supply those who are sick with whatever would be good for them, well then, you can visit them, you can say consoling words to them, you can pray for them so that they will put their illness to good use. Yes, my dear children, everything is good and precious in God's sight when we act from the motives of religion and of charity because Jesus Christ tells us that a glass of water would not go unrewarded. You see, therefore, my children, that although we may be quite poor, we can still easily give alms.

I told you that however exacting our work was, there is a certain kind of prayer which we can make continually without, at the same time, upsetting our labors, and this is how it is done. It is seeking, in everything we do, to do the will of God only. Tell me, my children, is it so difficult to seek only to do the will of God in all of our actions, however small they may be? Yes, my children, with that prayer everything becomes meritorious for Heaven, and without that will, all is lost. Alas! How many good things, which would help us so well to gain Heaven, go unrewarded simply by not doing our ordinary duties with the right intention!

౭ DO YOU WANT TO BE HAPPY?

WHY, MY DEAR BRETHREN, ARE OUR LIVES FULL OF so many miseries? If we consider the life of man carefully, it is nothing other than a succession of evils: the illnesses, the disappointments, the persecutions, and indeed the losses of goods fall unceasingly upon us so that whatever side the worldly man turns to or examines, he finds only crosses and afflictions. Go and ask anyone, from the humblest to the greatest, and they will all tell you the same thing. Indeed, my dear brethren, man on earth, unless he turns to the side of God, cannot be other than unhappy. Do you know why, my friends? No, you tell me. Well, here is the real reason.

It is that God, having put us into this world as into a place of exile and of banishment, wishes to force us, by so many evils, not to attach our hearts to it but to aspire to greater, purer, and more lasting joys than those we can find in this life. To make us appreciate more keenly the necessity to turn our eyes to eternal blessings, God has filled our hearts with desires so vast and so magnificent that nothing in creation is capable of satisfying them. Thus it is that in the hope of finding some pleasure, we attach ourselves to created objects and that we have no sooner possessed and sampled that which we have so ardently desired than we turn to something else, hoping to find what we wanted. We are, then, through our own experience, constrained to admit that it is but useless for us to want to derive our happiness here below from transient things. If we hope to have any consolation in this world, it will only be by despising the things which are passing and which have no lasting value and in striving towards the noble and happy end for which God has created us. Do you want to be happy, my friends? Fix your eyes on Heaven; it is there that your hearts will find that which will satisfy them completely.

All the evils which you experience are the real means of leading you there. That is what I am going to show you, in as clear and brilliant way as shines the noon-day sun. First of all, I am going to tell you that Jesus Christ, by His sufferings and His death, has made all our actions meritorious, so that for the good Christian there is no motion of our hearts or of our bodies which will not be rewarded if we perform them for Him.

Perhaps you are already thinking: "That is not so very clear." Very well! If that will not do you, let us put it more simply. Follow me for a moment and you will know the way in which to make all your actions meritorious for eternal life without changing anything in your way of behaving. All you have to do is to have in view the object of pleasing God in everything you do, and I will add that instead of making your actions more difficult by doing them for God, you will make them, on the contrary, much more pleasant and less arduous. In the morning, when you awake, think at once of God and quickly make the Sign of the Cross, saying to Him: "My God, I give you my heart, and since You are so good as to give me another day, give me the grace that everything I do will be for Your honor and for the salvation of my soul."

৪~ *THE GIFT OF EVERY DAY*

BEFORE BEGINNING YOUR WORK, MY DEAR BRETHREN, never fail to make the Sign of the Cross. Do not imitate those people without religion who dare not do this because they are in company. Offer quite simply all your difficulties to God and renew from time to time this offering, for by that means you will have the happiness of drawing down the blessing of Heaven on yourself and on all you do. Just think, my dear brethren, how many acts of virtue you can practice by behaving in this way, without making any change in what you are actually doing. If you work with the object of pleasing God and obeying His Commandments, which order you to earn your bread by the sweat of your brow, that is an act of obedience. If you want to expiate your sins, you are making an act of penance. If you want to obtain some grace for yourself or for others, it is an act of hope and of charity. Oh, how we could merit Heaven every day, my dear brethren, by doing just our ordinary duties, but by doing them for God and the salvation of our souls! Who stops you, when you hear the chimes striking, from thinking on the shortness of time and of saying in your minds: "Time passes and death comes closer. I am hastening towards eternity. Am I really ready to appear before the tribunal of God? Am I not in a state of sin?"

৪৯ *THE PUBLIC CROSSES*

I AM GOING TO TALK TO YOU NOW ABOUT THE PUBLIC crosses, and I am going to give you the reason for their number, for the blessings which flow from them, and for the great honor which the Church pays them. If our interior crosses are so numerous and if the public crosses, these images of that Cross on which our God died, are also so numerous, it is that we may have always present in our thoughts the reminder that we are the children of a crucified God.

We need not be surprised, my dear brethren, at the honor which the Church pays to this holy wood, which obtains for us so many graces and so many benefits. We see that the Church makes the Sign of the Cross in all her ceremonies, in the administration of all the Sacraments. Why is that? My friends, this is why. It is because all our prayers and all the Sacraments draw from the Cross their power and their virtue. During the Holy Sacrifice of the Mass, which is the greatest, the most solemn and the most sublime of all those actions which can glorify God, the priest makes the Sign of the Cross over and over again. God desires that we may never lose the memory of it as the surest means of our salvation and the most formidable instrument for repelling the Devil. He has created us in the form of a cross so that every man might be the image of this cross upon which Jesus Christ died to save us. See how eager the Church is to increase their number? She urges them as a special embellishment on our churches and on all altars; she places them in the most public places.

৪৯ *THE CROSSES WHICH ARE WORN*

WHY ARE CROSSES PLACED NEAR TOWNS AND VIL-lages? It is to show the public profession which the Christian should make of the religion of Jesus Christ and to remind all passers-by that they should never forget the memory of the Passion and death of our Savior. This sign of redemption distinguishes us from idolaters, as in olden times circumcision distinguished the Jewish people from the infidels. Let us note, too, that when people want to destroy religion, they begin by overturning these monuments.

The first Christians considered that their greatest happiness was to wear upon themselves this salutary sign of our Redemption. In other times, the women and girls wore a cross which they made their most precious ornament; they hung it around their necks, showing thereby that they were the servants of a crucified God. But progressively, as the Faith diminished and as religion became weakened, this sacred sign has become rare or, to be more precise, has practically disappeared. Notice how the Devil works gradually towards evil. In this matter it began by the cutting out of the image of the Crucified and of the Blessed Virgin, and by the wearers' being satisfied with a cross which had been converted into ornamental forms. After that the Devil pushed the matter further: to replace this sacred sign, a chain was chosen, which was nothing more nor less than an ornament of vanity and which, very far from drawing down blessings from Heaven upon the wearers, involved them only in the ways and the traps of the Devil. Look at the difference between a chain and a cross. By the Cross, we have become children of freedom; by the Cross, Jesus has delivered us from the tyranny of the Devil into which sin had led us. The chain, on the contrary, is a sign of slavery; in other words, by means of this token of vanity, we leave God and give ourselves over to the Devil. Lord! How the world has changed since the time of the first Christians.

Ah, how large is the number of those who are no longer Christians except in name and whose conduct resembles that of the pagans!

Ah, you will say to me, that is a bit strong now! We are not sorry that we are Christians; on the contrary. Tell us what you mean by saying that we have no more than the name of Christians.

Well, my friends, that is very easy. It is because you are afraid to perform your acts of religion in front of other people and that, when you are in a house, you do not dare to make the Sign of the Cross before eating, or else that, in order to make it, you will turn away so that you will not be noticed and laughed at. It is because, when you hear the Angelus ringing, you pretend not to have heard it and you do not say it for fear of someone making fun of you; or again, it is when God puts into your mind the thought of going to Confession and you say: "Oh, I am not going. They would be laughing at me." If you behave in this manner, you cannot say that you are Christians. No, my friends, you are, like those Jews of long ago, rejected or, rather, you have separated yourselves. You are nothing but apostates. Your language proves it, and your way of living manifests it equally clearly. Why, my dear brethren, was the name of apostate given to the Emperor Julian?

It was given to him, you will tell me, because he was a Christian to begin with but later he lived as the pagans do.

Well, then, my good friends, what difference is there between your conduct and that of the pagans? Do you know what the ordinary vices of the pagans are? Some, corrupted by the hideous vice of impurity, spew from their mouths all sorts of abominations; others, given over to gluttony, seek only tasty food or to fill themselves with wine. The sole preoccupation of their young girls is with clothes and the desire to look attractive to others. What do you think of conduct like that, my dear brethren?

That is the conduct of people who entertain no hope of any other life.

You are quite right. And what difference is there between your life and theirs? If you want to speak frankly, you will admit that there is none and that as a consequence, you are Christians in name only.

Oh, my God! that You have so few Christians to imitate You! Alas! If there are so few of them to wear their cross there will be only few, too, to bless You for all eternity.

☙ HARVEST CROSSES

BLESSED CROSSES ARE PUT IN THE FIELDS OR IN OPEN spaces, in places where a crop will be harvested. The purpose of the blessing is to implore God not to turn His merciful eyes away from the fields where they are placed but to spread His blessings there. That, however, is not all there is to planting crosses. It must be done with reverence, with faith, and, above all, it must not be done in a state of sin. You may be quite sure that if you plant them with the right sentiments, God will bless your lands and preserve them from temporal harm. If your crosses do not produce the effect which you should expect from them, it is not difficult to imagine that it is because you went to plant them without faith and without religion. It is because, when you were planting them, you did not perhaps say even an *Our Father* or a *Hail Mary* on your knees. Or that, if you did say your prayers, it was possibly with one knee only on the ground. If that is the case, how do you expect God to bless your harvest? But when you find them again . . . that is indeed another abomination! . . . Oh, my God! In what a dreadful age do we live! . . .

When the Church instituted this holy ceremony, everyone longed for the happiness of placing these crosses in his field and behaved with the utmost respect. When they were found, either during the reaping or the vintage, people bowed down to the earth to adore Jesus Christ, Who died on the Cross for us, and in that way they expressed their recognition of the fact that He had desired to bless and preserve their harvest. All, with tears in their eyes, kissed the sacred sign of our Redemption. Alas, my God, that it is no longer in that way that Christians recognize You!

Instead of expressing your gratitude to God for having graciously blessed and preserved the fruits of the earth, do you not, rather, offer Him an insult by laughing when you are kissing the cross? Is it not performing an act of derision, or rather of idolatry, to offer a handful of corn as if you were incensing the person who is holding the cross?

Carry on, unhappy sinners, God will punish you, either in this world or in the next! Fathers of families, have I not been telling you for the past two years that when the time comes for the reaping you should gather up all the crosses which are in your fields in order to save them from profanation? Have I not suggested to you to put them together in your barns and, when you have threshed your corn, to burn them, lest they be profaned? If you have not done that, you are very much to blame, and you must not omit to mention it in Confession. Alas! There is no counting all the horrible things which are done at the time of the harvest or of the vintage, at those very times when God, in His abundance and His love, covers the earth with the gifts of His providence! Ungrateful man seems at that time to redouble his insults and to multiply his crimes. How have you the impertinence to grumble if your harvests are short because the hail or the frost have harmed some of them? Ah, much rather should you be very surprised that, in spite of all your many sins, God still wants to give you the necessities of life and even more than is necessary too! Oh! My God! How mean and blind man is! . . .

ॐ THE ARMED CROSSES

THE SIGN OF THE CROSS IS THE MOST TERRIBLE weapon against the Devil. Thus the Church wishes not only that we should have it continually in front of our minds to recall to us just what our souls are worth and what they cost Jesus Christ, but also that we should make it at every juncture ourselves: when we go to bed, when we awaken during the night, when we get up, when we begin any action, and, above all, when we are tempted. We can say that a Christian who makes the Sign of the Cross with genuine religious sentiments, that is to say, when fully aware of the action which he is performing, makes all Hell tremble. But when we make the Sign of the Cross, we must make it not by habit but with respect, with attention and thinking of what we are doing. Ah, dear Lord, with what devout awe we should be filled when we make the Sign of the Cross upon ourselves and recall that we are pronouncing all that we hold holy and most sacred in our religion!

ଛ THE BELOVED CROSSES

THE SAINTS, MY DEAR BRETHREN, ALL LOVED THE Cross and found in it their strength and their consolation.

But, you will say to me, is it necessary, then, always to have something to suffer? . . . Now sickness or poverty, or again scandal or calumny, or possibly loss of money or an infirmity?

Have you been calumniated, my friends? Have you been loaded with insults? Have you been wronged? So much the better! That is a good sign; do not worry; you are on the road that leads to Heaven. Do you know when you ought to be really upset? I do not know if you understand it, but it should be precisely for the opposite reason—when you have nothing to endure, when everyone esteems and respects you. Then you should feel envious of those who have the happiness of passing their lives in suffering, or contempt, or poverty. Are you forgetting, then, that at your Baptism you accepted the Cross, which you must never abandon until death, and that it is the key that you will use to open the door of Heaven? Are you forgetting the words of our Savior: "If any man will come after me, let him deny himself, and take up his cross daily, and follow me." Not for a day, not for a week, not for a year, but all our lives. The saints had a great fear of passing any time without suffering, for they looked upon it as time lost. According to St. Teresa, man is only in this world to suffer, and when he ceases to suffer, he should cease to live. St. John of the Cross asks God, with tears, to give him the grace to suffer more as a reward for all his labors.

What should we conclude, my dear children, from all that? Just this: Let us make a resolution to have a great respect for all the crosses, which are blessed, and which represent to us in a small way all that our God Suffered for us. Let us recall that from the Cross flow all the graces that are bestowed upon us and that as a consequence, a cross which is blessed is a source of blessings, that we should often make the Sign of the Cross on ourselves and always with great respect, and, finally, that our houses should never remain without this symbol of salvation.

Fill your children, my dear brethren, with the greatest respect for the Cross, and always have a blessed cross on yourselves; it will protect you against the Devil, from the vengeance of Heaven, and from all danger. This is what I desire for you.

૨૭ *AFTERWORD*

ANYONE ANALYZING M. VIANNEY'S LIBRARY—THE
furniture and the books are still there, exactly as he left them
when he died—can see for himself that sermons figure largely
among his books, as do also works of theology and Sacred
Scripture.[1] The Curé of Ars was certainly preoccupied with
the idea of "asserting himself" as a preacher. Undoubtedly he
passed over the oratorical work of Bossuet of which there is no
sign at all among his books. He did possess an *Advent* by Bour-
dalue . . . But it is clear that in his choice of authors he was not
influenced in the slightest degree by literary considerations. In
the fairly frequent trips which he made to Lyons at the beginning of his pastorate, when he was renewing the vestments for
his poor little church, the Abbé Vianney did not content himself with visits to the goldsmiths and embroiderers alone; he
went to the bookshops. The house of Rusand, well known at
this period, had much of his custom. He bought books there
that had been recommended to him or which he personally
picked out. In that way he had at his disposal quite a considerable number of works to help him in composing his Sunday al-
locutions. It remains to be seen how much he drew from them.

The Bible is the first of the books which should not only be
consulted but studied by every preacher worthy of the name.
"He must," in the opinion of St. Augustine, "have read and
studied the whole of Sacred Scripture; he must reread it continually, because it is like those inexhaustible mines where there
are always new treasures to be found proportionate to what is
dug for, or like those exquisite pictures in which one always
discovers new beauties as one studies them more."[2] The Fathers
of the Church, and in particular St. John Chrysostom among
the Greeks, and St. Augustine among the Latins, have impreg-
nated their discourses with phrases and images borrowed from
the Bible. Among ourselves the preachers of the *grand siècle,*

183

and Bossuet above all, have made frequent and most felicitous use of it. All exponents of sacred eloquence have had a thorough knowledge of the holy Book.

The use which the Curé of Ars made of the Bible bears witness to his fairly extensive knowledge of the Scriptures, and, above all, of the Gospels.

His quotations are often made largely from memory; so it happens—very rarely, it is true—that M. Vianney gives his references incorrectly. He will attribute to the "holy Prophet-King" a text drawn from *Ecclesiasticus*, and to St. Paul a quotation from an unknown author. He will confuse the chastisement which threatened Nineveh with that which overtook Sodom. He will send the Prophet Habacuc "to carry food to the three children who were in the furnace of Babylon" while Habacuc fulfilled this task for Daniel thrown into the den of lions. But these are negligible errors.

In general, M. Vianney does not set out to quote Scripture as such. He develops, he arranges, he embellishes the inspired quotation; or, if he seems to render it in its native simplicity, he makes a really personal translation of it.

Together with Holy Scripture the Abbé Vianney had studied theology. What he learnt of it in the seminary of St. Irenaeus in Lyons hardly counted; M. Bailey, at the presbytery of Ecully, where the future Curé of Ars spent seven to eight years, was his unique teacher in the study of the sacred sciences. He was not only a saintly priest but he also had a most cultured mind: the diocesan administrators had offered him the professorship of moral theology in the seminary at Lyons but he had preferred to consecrate himself to the pastoral ministry. He took on the task of teaching his pupil the clear and solid dogmatic principles. He prepared him for his role of confessor and spiritual director by teaching him the current moral theology, that theological practice which came in a direct line from the eighteenth century and which showed itself so difficult in the matter of approach to the Sacraments of Penance and the Eucharist, so severe on public sinners, on habitual sinners and on recidivists.

The teaching received in his clerical youth explains the rigorism of which M. Vianney gave evidence during the first fifteen or twenty years he spent in the parish of Ars. Moreover, in showing himself a severe moralist, he held to the tradition of the clergy of Belley, the older men of whom had followed, before the Revolution, the courses in the seminary of St. Irenaeus, composed on the order and according to the direction of Msgr. de Montazet. This manual, without directly professing Jansenism, does in fact reproduce its spirit. The work, published in 1780, was not altogether to the liking of M. Emery and his Sulpicians, who were charged with the curriculum of St. Irenaeus, but they continued to teach it "without changing anything of importance in it after taking the advice of Monsignor."[3]

Neither in advance of nor behind his clerical contemporaries in this, the Abbé Vianney availed himself of the theology of his time—not that, in Catholic theology, there is a time or a truth which may be admitted at one time and rejected at another. We would say simply that the Curé of Ars, when it was a matter of giving practical solutions from the pulpit, followed the customs he had been taught.

To most of his listeners he could have appeared very slightly "jansenist"[4] when he uttered in his first years such pronouncements as the following: "Alas! that Christians who leave the church (after assisting at Mass) have perhaps more than thirty or fifty mortal sins more than when they came in!" The preacher considered himself severe, for he formulated the objection which he sensed in the minds of the listeners: "But," you will say, "it would be much better not to assist at it then." And he replies with of shift of ground: "Do you know what you should do? You should assist at it, and assist at it as well as you can. . . ."

In the sermon on *The Thought of Death* he puts this despairing statement into the mouth of St. Jerome as he was dying: "I speak of it to you with the experience of more than sixty years. Yes, my dear children, of one hundred thousand people who have lived badly there will scarcely be one who will have a good death!" This is not, it is true, a quotation, but it is obvious that the Curé of Ars brought it in here with a certain amount of willingness.

In preaching to the fathers and mothers of families about their duties towards their children he made their duties appear so difficult that these poor people had to decide either not to fulfill them or to become saints.

It is absolutely essential to see in these doctrinal exaggerations either oratorical amplification or the desire to inspire in the souls (of his listeners) a salutary apprehension. "But," our saint makes an imaginary opponent say in his sermon on *The Delay in Conversion*, ". . . that would be enough to throw one into despair." "Ah! my friend," retorts the preacher, "I would like to be able to bring you to the edge of despair so that, struck by the terrifying state you are in, you would at least take the means that God offers you even to-day to get out of it."

M. Vianney, wishing to impress souls vigorously, had surely the need to "exaggerate" certain details of morality in order to make them more understandable to the least instructed portion of his audience. In addition, his austere temperament inclined him to preach the terrible truths: he returned, in almost every sermon, to the last end, to death, to judgment, to hell.

Experience in dealing with souls taught him to be a less stern moralist. However, as a missionary who heard him in his last years has said, he preserved right up to the end "a slight tendency to severity, when he was speaking with such energy on the threats of divine justice, on the terrors of the judgment, on hell." For he treated of all these frightening subjects as continually as ever when numerous pilgrims were mingling with the people of his parish.

Nevertheless, he never excluded from his theology the dogma of the divine mercy. We have a special sermon by him on that very consoling truth.[5] And "the preference which he gave to this theme in his later years clearly shows that it was the sentiment of the love of God which he wished to make predominate in souls."[6]

Many religious and priests, even bishops, sat among the simple faithful at the foot of his pulpit. "It is outrageous that anyone should reproach the Servant of God with the slightest inexactitude in doctrine, dogmatic or moral."[7]

M. Vianney possessed in his library the *Ecclesiastical History* by Fleury. He went through it and quoted it sometimes in his instructions, while taking care, at least on one occasion, to indicate the reference.

But the history book which he knew best and quoted most frequently, together with the Scriptures, was the *Lives of the Saints*. He finished by knowing it practically by heart. "It could be truly said that he had lived with these great saints, by the way he told about the details of their lives."[8] "Every day," testifies Catherine Lassagne, who had charge of his little household, "I found on the table this volume which I had put back in its place in the bookshelves the day before."[9] And Jeanne Marie Chanay, assistant at the orphanage of Mlle. Lassagne, adds: "The Curé never gave up this reading, not even at the period of the pilgrimage when he spent his day entirely in the confessional and returned home, in the evening, overwhelmed with fatigue."[10] The *Lives of the Saints*, in the full meaning of the word, was his bedside book.

And there is no doubt but that it was with his preaching in mind that he made this reading a strict rule, in addition to which he found in it rest and consolation. "He loved," recalls M. Pagès, who was living in retirement in the village of Ars, "to read over each evening the account of the saint whose feast it was the following day, and at his catechism at 11 o'clock, he told with delight what he had read the evening before."[11]

One of the books from which he took his edifying stories is still preserved in his library. It is indeed the only book, or one of the very few, on which he wrote his name—it seems that by that he wanted to mark the value which he attached to it. Made up of two enormous volumes of folio size, it is entitled *Lives of the Saints of whom the Office is said in the course of the year.* The author was Père François Giry, an old Provincial of the Order of Minims.[12] But it was not from this source that the Curé of Ars drew most. He often quoted Ribadeneira, whose book disappeared from his room. He borrowed from him six legends in the sermon on *The Death of the Just.* He accumulated up to seven copies of the old Spanish author from which to preach to the parishioners of Ars resistance to temptation.[13]

M. Vianney rarely quotes textually from Giry or from Ribadeneira. Generally he fits them in according to his plan, and sometimes in an original and charming way. Certain mistakes which he made indicate that, when writing, he had recourse less to his eyes than to his memory. He will attribute to St. Francis of Paula that poetic miracle of the *Sermon to the Fish* which was actually wrought by St. Anthony of Padua. He will write in the same place "See a St. John who commands the birds to be silent" while this gracious miracle of the birds belongs to St. Francis of Assisi.[14]

The Curé of Ars frequented the mystics.

He studied the *Holy Ladder* by St. John Climaque. He took from it not points of doctrine but examples—examples of humility or penitence.

He did not ignore the *Conference of the Fathers of the Desert* by Cassien. In his instruction *On Temptation,* he drew from this venerable work the long story of the old anchorite who passes through a terrible crisis of despair and learns thus to sympathize with the hidden trials of his brethren.

The *Practice of Christian Perfection* by Rodriguez seems to have had no secrets for the Curé of Ars. He had a translation of it by Regnier des Marais. However, he did not copy it at all: he took from it the "marrow and substance." One can see that, of works by this ascetic author, M. Vianney had especially studied the *Third Treatise* wherein there is a discussion of the three degrees of humility. The sermon which he composed on this fundamental virtue is inspired here and there by Rodriguez. In his instruction on *Abstinence and the Quarter Tense* he himself took the trouble, in the manuscript, to indicate his references: there are four of them which he refers to the *Practice of Perfection*. The explanations which he gives, in his *Sermon on the Holy Mass*, touching the symbolism of the sacerdotal adornments, come in direct line from Rodriguez.[15]

With regard to the authors of *sermons*, we have already hinted that M. Vianney procured their works for himself on the chance of finding something which might suit him. While he rarely copied them he borrowed from them fairly often, as also with his mannal of theology, the very foundation of his preaching. He made use almost exclusively of three books of sermons, namely: *The Missionary of the Oratory or Sermons chosen for Advent, Lent and the Feasts of the year in which are explained the principal Christian truths which are taught on the missions, drawn from Holy Scripture, the Councils and the Holy Fathers*, by Père Le Jeune, called the Blind Father, priest of the Oratory of Jesus; the *Sermons* of Messire Claude Joly, Bishop and Count d'Agen;[16] the *Familiar Instructions for evening prayer during Lent* and *Familiar Course of Instructions or the principal events of the Old Testament* by Canon Bonnardel of Autun. .

Nothing in the oratorical work of M. Vianney indicates that he had read the ten huge volumes which contain the sermons of Père Le Jeune. Nevertheless, it is this old preacher of the seventeenth century, contemporary of St. Francis de Sales and of St. Vincent de Paul[17] who has left the greatest impression on our Curé of Ars. He borrowed from him, as we shall see presently, certain ideas, barely two or three pages, but quite often he seems to be penetrated with his style. "Père Le Jeune," says a notice placed at the beginning of his works, "is simple, touching, insinuating; it can be seen that he was born with a happy spirit and a sensitive soul."[18] He is more realist in description and expression; the long word never frightened him. We shall say the same thing of M. Vianney. Then, there is in the Curé of Ars, to bring him close to Père Le Jeune, more than memories of reading. Each one of them, as one can easily establish by reading through their sermons, is of the same character—eager, ardent, quick-witted. While Père Le Jeune preached that Lent in Rouen where he lost his sight, several lords of the court arrived, who begged the Oratorian to give them his finest sermon. He contented himself with giving them a familiar instruction dealing with the duties of the great towards the king, and their obligations in respect of their families and of their servants. We shall see the humble Curé of Ars speak with the same integrity and the same simplicity in the presence of both Lacordaire and the ignorant villagers. The *Blind Father* debated very little on questions of dogma; he devoted himself almost entirely to attacking the abuses and the vices of his time. So here we have two popular preachers who resemble one another in a most remarkable way. M. Vianney undoubtedly adapted himself to his surroundings and his period, but his remonstrances, and his invectives are like an echo of Père Le Jeune speaking on the *Disorders of Sin*, the *Insults which the sinner offers to God*, on the *Judgment* and on an *Unhappy Eternity*.

In detail, the Curé of Ars borrowed from the old preacher at the very most certain legends—such, for example, as the violent death of the bookseller in Lorraine who was hanged by the Devil, the conversion of the courtesan Thais by the holy Abbé Paphnuce, the tragic adventure of Theophilus, deacon of Alexandria, who having signed a pact with Satan was finally saved by the Blessed Virgin. And again, these stories are made to suit both his text and his audience. Only on one occasion did M. Vianney allow himself to take a fairly long passage word for word from Père Le Jeune and that was touching the affection which the Blessed Virgin showed to the newly-born St. John the Baptist. Anyone reading through the *Sermons* of the

Curé of Ars will instantly notice this passage which is out of keeping with the rest, and will perceive its archaic and very different style.[19]

Claude Joly, Bishop of Agen, whose sermons Abbé Vianney studied very attentively, was not an orator on a great scale, but he was a vigorous dialectician and a solid theologian. He knew the Scriptures and the Fathers well and made excellent quotations from them. This bishop of the seventeenth century had truly apostolic accents. A preacher of our own period could still draw a great deal of useful material from his sermons which today are quite forgotten. "The homilies and the sermons of his which remain to us are often merely sketches, but one might say of these sketches what Virgil said of the works of the poet Ennius: that he had extracted gold from them."[20]

In default of gold the Curé of Ars extracted some excellent things from the oratorical works of Messire Claude Joly. He was, however, inspired by them only, without copying them in any servile way. He even imposed a considerable work on himself in adapting the text of a learned prelate to the capacity of his country congregation of listeners, in clarifying and freeing it from ancient or too abstruse expressions. He cut out anything which involved scholastic reasoning, or too subtle deductions. He kept, on the other hand and willingly, images and pictures drawn from Holy Scripture, and certain vivid and striking thoughts. But he undertook personally the practical application of them and in that he excelled; in a word, from a *discourse* of Messire Claude Joly, a discourse which might be a little stiff and remote, the Curé of Ars made a *popular sermon.*

The Curé of Ars preferred Canon Bonnardel of Autun even to Père Le Jeune or to Messire Claude Joly. It was to his *Familiar Instructions* that he had recourse most frequently to find the title and the subject for his Sunday sermons. After all, was not his whole aim simply to compose for his villagers *Familiar Instructions?* Generally, M. Vianney took the thought of Bonnardel rather than his expressions. He commented on the thought and added to it appropriate examples. One of his most original and vivid sermons—on the *Sanctification of the Christian*—belongs, for its source, to the *Instructions* of the Canon of Autun. What is more, it is specially to his parishioners of Ars, and not to any kind of listeners, that our holy preacher addresses himself: he thunders against the *winter gatherings* of Ars, against "all those sins which have been committed in your outhouses and stables during the five or six months of winter"; he attacks the blasphemers of Ars, the cabarets and those who give them a livelihood: it is a picture of customs and behavior bearing a very individual character.

If, therefore, the Curé of Ars, in the fever of a superhuman labour, allowed himself fairly numerous borrowings from several pulpit orators, it is none the less certain that his personal contribution to the major portion of his sermons far outweighed the borrowings.

MSGR. FRANÇOIS TROCHU

NOTES

1. We were able to make this list in the actual library of the Saint. Here are the titles of a certain number of his books. The comparatively recent date indicates that they were personally acquired by the Curé of Ars and were not the legacy of M. Balley, Curé of Ecully, who had left him his books.
List:
Course of Sermons by a Large Number of French Ecclesiastical Refugees in Germany during the Persecution. (2 Vols. 12mo. Leclère, Paris, 1816.)
Sermons of Messire Claude Joly, Bishop and Count of Agen. (4 Vols. 12mo., at the expense of the Society, Avignon, 1741.)
Sermons arranged for the Sundays and Principal Feasts of

the Year, by M. Billot, former director of the Seminary at Besançon. (Belin, Paris, 1802.)

Sermons of Père de Ligny, Life of Our Lord Jesus Christ. (2 Vols. 12mo. Périsse, Lyons, 1820.)

Familiar Instructions for Night Prayers during Lent by Bonnardel, Canon of Autun. (Rusand, Lyons, 1823.)

Course of Familiar Instructions or the Principal Events of the Old Testament and Six Sermons on the Summary of the Truths of the Faith and Morality. By the same author. (8 Vols. 12mo. Rusand, Lyons, 1818-1819.)

The Voice of the Pastor, Familiar Discourses of a Curé by M. Regis. (2 Vols. 12mo. Laurent Aubanel, Avignon, 1823.)

People's Catechisms of the Country and the Towns by a Missionary Priest. (2 Vols. 12mo. Pélagaud, Lyons, 1844.)

Simple Talks, in Catechism Form, of a Country Pastor with the Young People, called the Constance Catechism. (4 Vols. 12mo. Rusand, Lyons, 1828.)

Catechism, Dogmatic and Moral. (4 Vols. Lagier, Dijon, 1825.)

Catéchisme de Couturier. (4 Vols. 12mo. Lagier, Dijon, 1825.)

Treatise on the Holy Mysteries by M. Collat. (2 Vols. 12mo. Méquignon, 1823.)

Ritual of Toulon, Instructions on the Ritual. (Chamberu, Paris, 1822.)

Conferences of Angers. (24 Vols. 12mo. Gacun, Paris, 1829.)

Dictionary of Theology, Bergier. (8 Vols. 8vo. Douladoure, Toulouse, 1823.)

The City of God: St. Augustine. (Gille, Bourges, 1818.)

Chosen Stories. (Douladoure, Toulouse, 1816.)

Holy Bible, with Commentaries by Ménochius. (15 Vols. 8vo. Rusand, Lyons.)

2. M. Hamon. *Treatise on Preaching*, op. cit., p. 213.

3. Abbé Gosselin, *Life of M. Emery*, Jouby, Paris, 1862, t.I, pp. 208-209.

4. Here the term "jansenist" is used in the sense of "rigorist" and nothing more. In fact, the Curé of Ars detested Jansenism. In 1827 he refused the offer to be appointed Curé of Fareins because there were in this parish "too many bourgeois and pagans." By these words he designated the Jansenist sect which

in Fareins comprised half of the population. (Abbé Rougemont, *Apostolic Process continuative*, p. 751.)

5. Cf. "You Are Surprised, But Not I!" (For the 2nd Sunday after Pentecost).

6. Abbé Dufour, *Apostolic Process, in genere*, p. 339.

7. *Apostolic Process, ne pereant*, p. 1293.

8. Baroness de Belvey. *Ordinary's Process*, p. 236.

9. *Ordinary's Process*, p. 507.

10. *Ordinary's Process*, p. 700. The Curé of Ars must also have read the *Lives of the Saints* while taking his meals. The two volumes by Giry, which are still in his room, have bread-crumbs on many of their pages.

11. *Ordinary's Process*, p. 431.

12. Imbert, Paris, 1703.

13. Cf. "The Bad Death" (4th Sunday of Lent).

14. Cf. "If Man Knew His Religion" (14th Sunday after Pentecost).

15. *Practice of Christian Perfection* by Alphonse Rodriguez. New translation, Dézallier, Paris, 1688, t.II, p. 580.

16. The sermons of Claude Joly were inserted in the *Integral and Universal Collection of Sacred Orators* by Migne, (Ed. Gaume) in tome XXXII; those of Père Le Jeune in tomes III, IV and V.

17. Born in 1592, Jean Le Jeune was one of the first disciples of Bérulle at the Oratory. Becoming blind at the age of 33 while he was preaching the Lenten sermons at Rouen, he retired to Limoges, where he died in 1672 aged 80. Massillon valued his sermons very highly. St. Benedict Labre, who was in Dardilly, the birthplace of the Curé of Ars, as a guest of the Vianney's, had, it is said, derived from the reading of Père Le Jeune a little of the heroic courage which he displayed in the practice of the Christian virtues. The sermons of the *Blind Priest* have had many editions, notably those of Toulouse, 1662; of Paris, 1671; of Lyons, 1823-1827; of Clermont, 1838.

18. Edition by Clermont, t.I, introd., p. VIII.

19. It is a question of the sermon by M. Vianney for the feast of St. John the Baptist. The accent of this sermon is truly personal; one may ask why the Curé had put into his text a portion taken from the sermon on the Birth, Life and Death of St. John the Baptist by Père Le Jeune (t.XII, pp. 134-125). Phrases like these are certainly not in his style: "What purity

Mary must have communicated to St. John the Baptist, in ca-
ressing him, in embracing him, in bestowing on his lips the
spirit of the grace of her own virginal breath; for in this moment Jesus and Mary were, so to speak, but one person: Jesus,
in those happy times for Mary, breathed only through Mary's
mouth; the breath of Mary was but the respiration of Jesus."

20. *Correspondence of a former director of a seminary with
a young priest.* (No author's name.) Lesne, Lyons, 1842, p. 129.

If you have enjoyed this book, consider making your next selection from among the following . . .